Heart SONGS

To dearest Peggy, Jack and Kaitlin...

Heart Songs

A Family Treasury of True Stories of
Hope and Inspiration

With Love & Blessings Always! ♡

KATHRYN SLATTERY

Kathryn Slattery

☺, XO

Inspiring Voices
A Service of **Guideposts**

Heart Songs

Copyright © 2012 Kathryn Slattery

All rights reserved. No part of this book may be used or reproduced by any means, graphic, electronic, or mechanical, including photocopying, recording, taping or by any information storage retrieval system without the written permission of the publisher except in the case of brief quotations embodied in critical articles and reviews.

Cover layout and design by Laura Kagemann.
Interior layout and design by Christian Kelly.

Inspiring Voices books may be ordered through booksellers or by contacting:

Inspiring Voices
1663 Liberty Drive
Bloomington, IN 47403
www.inspiringvoices.com
1-(866) 697-5313

Because of the dynamic nature of the Internet, any web addresses or links contained in this book may have changed since publication and may no longer be valid. The views expressed in this work are solely those of the author and do not necessarily reflect the views of the publisher, and the publisher hereby disclaims any responsibility for them.

Any people depicted in stock imagery provided by Thinkstock are models, and such images are being used for illustrative purposes only. Certain stock imagery © Thinkstock.

ISBN: 978-1-4624-0030-0 (sc)
ISBN: 978-1-4624-0029-4 (e)

Library of Congress Control Number: 2011941950

Printed in the United States of America

Inspiring Voices rev. date: 12/6/2011

For story lovers everywhere

Acknowledgments

Every attempt has been made to credit the sources of copyrighted material used in this book. If any such acknowledgment has been inadvertently omitted or misattributed, receipt of such information would be appreciated.

The Gospel for Kids was originally published by Chariot Books, David C. Cook Publishing Company, Copyright © 1989 by Kathryn Slattery.

Grandma I'll Miss You: A Child's Story of Death and New Life was originally published by Chariot Books, David C. Cook Publishing Company, Copyright © 1993 by Kathryn Slattery.

Emmett McCallister's Christmas Eve: An Old Tale Retold, by Kathryn Slattery, appears with permission from Guideposts Books, Copyright © 1980 by Guideposts, New York, NY 10016.

The following chapters in this book originally appeared in whole, or in part, or in some similar version, in *Guideposts* magazine, Copyright © 2002 by Guideposts, New York, NY 10016, and appear with permission:

"Moving Day" by Kathryn Slattery, originally appeared as "Sincerely..." *Guideposts*, May 1983.

"City Sunset" by Kathryn Slattery, originally appeared as "Fragile Moments ... When God Speaks in Whispers," *Guideposts*, July 1985.

"Family Forever" by Kathryn Slattery, originally appeared as "Brin(c)kerhoffs Forever!" *Guideposts*, October 1986.

"Mirror, Mirror" by Kathryn Slattery, originally appeared as "Out of Molasses Swamp," *Guideposts*, September 1986.

"How to Re-Charge Your Churchgoing" by Kathryn Slattery, originally appeared as "How to: Get Your Churchgoing Going Again," *Guideposts*, April 1989.

"Liberty Weekend" by Kathryn Slattery, originally appeared as "Afterglow," *Guideposts*, July 1987.

"Ah, Summertime" by Kathryn Slattery, originally appeared as "Sincerely..." *Guideposts*, July 1992.

"All I Want for Christmas" by Kathryn Slattery, originally appeared as "Kitty's Crown," *Guideposts*, December 1990.

"My Christmas Angel" by Kathryn Slattery, originally appeared as "Sincerely..." *Guideposts*, December 1986.

"How to Be a Great Godparent" by Kathryn Slattery, originally appeared as "Godmother," *Guideposts*, January 1990.

"How to Make Easter Real for Your Kids" by Kathryn Slattery, originally appeared as "How to: Make the Real Easter Real for Your Kids," *Guideposts*, April 1992.

"Homecoming" by Kathryn Slattery, originally appeared as "Getting the Message at Last," *Guideposts*, November 1993.

"I Like You Just the Way You Are," by Fred Rogers with Kathryn Brinckerhoff (Slattery), originally appeared in *Guideposts*, September 1980.

"The Six Pence" by Kathryn Slattery, originally appeared as "Mother of the Bride," *Guideposts*, June 2011, Copyright © 2011 by Guideposts.

The following chapters in this book are adapted from *Lost & Found: One Daughter's Story of Amazing Grace*, Guideposts Books, Copyright © 2008 by Kathryn Slattery:

"Motherhood... A New Kind of Love"
"The Dancing Lesson"
"Lost and Found"
"The Black Dress"

Unless otherwise indicated, Scripture quotations are taken from *The Holy Bible, New International Version*® Copyright © 1973, 1978, 1984 by International Bible Society. All rights reserved.

Other Scripture quotations are taken from the following sources: *The Holy Bible: Revised Standard Version* (RSV). Copyright © 1946, 1952, 1973 by National Council of Churches of Christ. All rights reserved. *The King James Version* (KJV) Public domain.

"Take hope, for writing is magic. Even the simplest act of writing is almost supernatural, on the borderline with telepathy. Just think: We can make a few abstract marks on a piece of paper in a certain order and someone a world away and a thousand years from now can know our deepest thoughts. The boundaries of space and time and even the limitations of death can be transcended ... Our stories have the power to heal, to make the world new again, to give people metaphors by which they can better understand their own lives."

—Christopher Vogler, *The Writer's Journey*

Contents

Note to Reader xiii

Acknowledgments xvii

Motherhood ... a New Kind of Love 1

Moving Day 7

City Sunset 9

Katy's Kingdom 11

Family Forever! 15

Mirror, Mirror 20

The Broken Vase 24

How to Recharge Your Churchgoing 27

Liberty Weekend 30

Ah, Summertime 35

Chicken Pox! 37

How to Grow Your Child's Faith in God 41

The Gospel for Kids 47

How to Give Good Gifts to Your Kids at Christmastime 55

All I Want for Christmas 59

Emmett McCallister's Christmas Eve: An Old Tale Retold 63

My Christmas Angel 70

How to Be a Great Godparent 72

How to Make Easter Real for Your Kids 77

Grandma, I'll Miss You: A Child's Story about Death and New Life 81

Homecoming 91

My Secret Garden 94

Dad's Flag 96

The Power of Human Kindness 102

Important Things: In Memoriam, September 11, 2001 105

Waiting for the Call 109

Dear God: *Help!* An Anxious Mother's Conversation with God 112

Prayer for a Teenage Son 114

How to Say Good-Bye to Worry 115

Out of Empty Nest Valley 119

The Dancing Lesson 123

New Year's Reflection on "Perfection" 128

Holy Smoke! The Amazing Story of How I Quit Smoking 131

Lost and Found 135

The Black Dress 141

The Butterfly's Secret 145

Squeezed in the Middle: How to Care for an Aging Parent in the Sandwich Generation 149

Counting My Blessings on Mother's Day 157

Max and the Lost Keys 161

Learning to Let Go in a "Tiger Mom" World 167

Prayer for Adult Children 170

The Sixpence 171

Tired of Junk E-Mails? *Send This Story to Every Woman You Know!* ... 178

My Favorite Interview: Fred Rogers, "I Like You Just the Way You Are" 182

What's Your Story? Kitty's Writing Tips 189

Heart Song. 193

About the Author 195

Note to Reader

Dear Reader,

I've been writing true first-person stories for going on four decades—as a long-time contributing editor for *Guideposts* magazine, memoirist, and the author of several books for children—and every day I continue to be amazed at the incredible *power* of the true, first-person narrative to reach out and touch the human heart.

The truth is, we are all storytellers. Indeed, there are many who believe that the desire and ability to tell stories is the primary characteristic of being *human*. There's a reason God made us this way. When we choose to step out in faith, take a risk, and share our stories—whether around the dinner table with our family, over a cup of coffee with a friend, or through the pages of a book—beautiful and amazing things can happen. Through the power of God's grace, our hearts are opened. We realize we are not alone in our various human frailties, fears, and failures. We appreciate in a new way how much we need each other. In a word, we *connect*. Through that connection, our hearts are mysteriously touched. We experience an increased capacity to empathize, forgive, and love. As a good friend once told me, "Kitty, the reason God put us here on earth is to help each other. One of the best ways we do this is by sharing our stories."

When it comes to life, I am no expert. Perhaps, like you, I'm just a regular mom, daughter, sister, wife, and friend—struggling each day to appreciate and not take for granted the good and joyful moments in life, while at the same time trying to learn lessons from and somehow make sense of life's heartaches, disappointments, and unexpected challenges.

I read somewhere once that the world is a broken place made up of broken people, and because of this, we sometimes cut ourselves on the broken pieces. At first this might seem a discouraging way of looking at life. But if there's one thing I've learned as a person of faith, it's that while we may, indeed, begin life born broken into a broken world, what life is *about* is the transformational journey of being gently and tenderly put back together by our loving God. It is about *being made whole*. This restorative, healing process doesn't happen all at once, but gradually … season by season … day by day … one insight at a time. Over the years, I've come to think of these incremental spiritual discoveries, these mini-epiphanies, these life-affirming "Aha!" moments when God sings His tender melody of hope and healing in our hearts as *heart songs*… Hence, the title of this book.

When you stop to think about it, the stories of our lives are a lot like songs—beautiful, eternal songs composed by our loving God. Here on earth, especially during times of trial, we struggle to comprehend the Composer's intentions. Indeed, there are dark times when we cannot hear His song at all. Our hearts are silent. "For now we see through a glass darkly," the apostle Paul wrote, "but then in heaven, face to face. For now on earth I know in part—but then, in heaven, I shall know fully—even as I am also fully known" (1 Corinthians 13:12, KJV).

But even with our human limitations, there are moments on earth when heaven breaks through and we hear with breathtaking clarity a completed stanza of our life's song. We are forgiven and discover that we can forgive. We are loved and discover that we can love. We are saved … set free … healed … reconciled. When such amazing moments of grace occur, we marvel at their beautiful harmony and perfect rhyme. We sense the Composer's loving presence. We hear His gentle voice resonate in our hearts like a perfectly pitched tuning fork, and in response our spirits sing out with deep meaning, purpose, faith, and hope.

In heaven, God promises that we will see and hear everything clearly. In heaven, everything will finally make sense. The good and loving Composer will take His children by the hand and show us how all the heartache, troubles, loss, and tears of this earthly life were just unfinished stanzas of our songs waiting to be rhymed with the miraculous ink of His redemptive grace. In heaven God will show us how nothing in life goes to waste. He will show us how everything in life—even pain— has value and how something beautiful and good can rise from the rubble of life's most difficult circumstances and mistakes. From illness, He will show us His beautiful song of healing ... from addiction, a song of deliverance ... from a hardened heart, a song of compassion ... from hurts and misunderstandings, a song of forgiveness ... and from estrangement, a song of reconciliation.

But we are not in heaven—not quite yet. So for now, we incline our ears and listen—carefully—for those divine and fleeting moments when heaven's music breaks through and our hearts sing in perfect harmony with our loving God.

It is my fondest hope and prayer that this book will serve as a powerful source of hope, encouragement, and inspiration for you and your family. May God be with you as you read, and may your heart be touched and your life eternally transformed by His gentle, loving grace.

With blessings always,

Kitty

Visit Kitty and learn more about her work at her website:
www.KathrynSlattery.com
and her Facebook Author Page:
Kathryn "Kitty" Slattery

Acknowledgments

This book is written for my family, with eternal love and gratitude to my husband, Tom, and to our children, Katy and Brinck. It is also written in loving memory of Elizabeth Mae Johnson Brinckerhoff and John Gilbert Brinckerhoff, the best parents in the world.

Katy and me, Minnetonka, Minnesota

Motherhood ... a New Kind of Love

When my husband Tom and I phoned my mother with the happy news of our daughter Katy's birth, she flew out to visit us right away. During her five-day visit to our home in Minnetonka, Minnesota, she insisted on answering the telephone and told people who called that I was "resting"—even when I wasn't. She said that phone calls and too many visitors would tire me out. That's what had happened to her, she said, when I was born.

She bought bags and bags of groceries and prepared a month's supply of casseroles that she wrapped in aluminum foil and carefully labeled with her elegant curlicue Palmer Method penmanship—*Jones Sausage Casserole, Buttonwood Casserole, Tuna Puff Casserole*—before pushing them into the crowded freezer. She *oohed* and *aahed* at baby gifts the postman delivered—pink hand-knitted booties, a miniature pair of rosebud-print OshKosh B'Gosh overalls, and a fuzzy, pastel menagerie of stuffed ducks, turtles, frogs, and teddy bears.

And when she picked her new granddaughter up, her eyes shone in a way I'd never seen before—at least not that I could remember.

"Such a *good* little girl," she cooed.

After my mother returned home and I was alone holding my new daughter, I heard myself cooing the exact same words with the exact same intonation.

"Such a *good* little girl ..."

There were nursery rhymes, too, that seemed to materialize from out of nowhere.

"Ride a cock-horse to Banbury Cross," I bounced Katy on my knee and chanted in a new, yet oddly familiar sing-songy voice. "To see a fine lady upon a white horse ... With rings on her fingers and bells on her toes ... She shall have music wherever she goes!"

Where in the world did that come from? I wondered.

It was as though the words and songs, like seeds, had been planted long ago. And now, as naturally and miraculously as the warm sun on a gentle spring day, my baby daughter was coaxing them to emerge, like tender green shoots out of the darkness.

Weeks later, Katy was cradled in my left arm, napping. She looked like a plump, furled flower bud. But on this particular summer afternoon, with every heat and humidity record being broken, I felt no rosy raptures of motherhood. Hot, tired, crabby, and frustrated was more like it.

Earlier in the day, my mother phoned and asked, "So, how's the baby? Is everything under control?"

Under control? I thought.

The day before, my goal had been ridiculously simple: to make tuna salad. Early in the morning I had set out the necessary ingredients and utensils: two cans of tuna fish, a bunch of celery, jar of mayonnaise, salt, pepper, stainless steel mixing bowl, can opener, and spoon. Now, twenty-four hours later, they were all still sitting there on the kitchen counter, untouched.

Under control?

"Yeah, Mom," I replied. "Everything's under control. The baby's doing fine."

"Great!" she said. "That's all I wanted to hear."

I hung up the phone, grateful that my daughter was doing fine. But as for me—I wasn't so sure. For the first eight weeks of Katy's life, my life had been reduced to a monotonous round of changing diapers, waking three times a night for feedings, soothing her cries—and worrying.

How could I know for sure what my daughter's cries meant?
Is she hungry? Lonely? Sick? Or just uncomfortable from the heat?

The new car seat, stroller, and baby swing had all come with pages of instructions. If only my new baby did too!

Now, after twenty minutes of fussing, Katy had finally drifted off in the crook of my arm. I sat at the dining room table, my free right hand busily scribbling the first of scores of long-overdue thank-you notes. An unfamiliar noise caused me to look up.

Cruncha-cruncha-cruncha.

Across the room, our calico cat Indy nibbled at the leaves of my one healthy potted plant.

How I wanted to yell a loud, outraged, *"Scat!"* How I ached to jump up off my chair and chase the cat. But to do so would wake my sleeping baby. I was stuck—trapped. Frustrated beyond belief, my fingers closed around the ballpoint pen in my hand, and I flung it toward the cat. It hit the wall above the plant and clattered to the floor. Regarding me coolly, Indy continued to nibble the green leaves.

Ashamed, I sat very still and squeezed my eyes shut. Warm drops ran into the corners of my mouth, and I took a shaky breath.

Oh, God, I prayed silently. *That wasn't very grown-up of me, was it? Sometimes being a mother makes me feel overwhelmed—helpless.*

I leaned back in the chair and studied my baby girl—this tiny, fragile bud of a human being. My daughter. I remembered so clearly the feeling that came over me the night Tom and I brought Katy home from the hospital. Together we leaned on the rail of her crib and watched her sleeping soundly in her new home for the first time. I looked at that sweet face, the perfectly modeled fingers and toes, and the petite upturned nose, and felt millions of tiny dancing bubbles well up inside of me—a different kind of love. It was not like my love for Tom. Or my father. Or my mother. Or my sister. This love was newborn, like my baby. Unlike anything I'd ever felt before, it filled me with a fierce tenderness. I would do anything to protect this tiny creature, so dependent on me for her life.

The memory was good, like a gentle hand taking mine. And as I looked down on my sleeping daughter, a new thought dawned.

Without You, God, I'm as helpless and dependent as my child. But You take care of me, giving me the strength to take care of her.

Weeks passed. It was late in the summer now, and the heat wave had broken. I was in the basement loading clothes into the dryer. Katy was upstairs asleep in her crib. Suddenly I heard her cry. There was an anguished note to it, as though she felt utterly abandoned. I slammed the dryer door shut, dashed up the stairs, and wrapped her in my arms.

"There, there," I crooned, holding her close to my breast, the soft curve of her head nesting perfectly in the hollow under my chin. "Please don't cry. Mommy's here. Mommy's always here. I'll never leave you, my little Katy."

Together we settled into the bentwood rocker and relaxed in its soothing rhythm. *Back and forth ... back and forth ... back and forth ...* until, like a gentle breeze, the words came to me—God's promise to *His* children: "Lo, I am with you always" (Matthew 28:20, KJV).

Dear God, I thought, *You always hear me when I cry too. You are always there, aren't You?*

The long Minnesota winter passed, and Katy was beginning to walk. Sitting cross-legged on the grassy lawn, I watched my intrepid explorer start up the steps leading to the wooden deck at the back of the apartment. At the base of the steps was a slab of poured concrete. Poised on the first step, Katy turned to face me, her eyes shining with pride in her accomplishment. But her legs, unsteady, began to wobble.

Even before I moved to catch her, I knew I was too late. Down she went, face-first, whacking her forehead on the concrete.

"*Katy!*"

Her brow was scraped and bleeding, already purple with an ugly bruise. She was screaming, and as I picked her up, nightmarish fears darkened my mind. *Concussion ... skull fracture ... brain damage ...*

Still carrying her, I raced up the steps and into our bedroom, where the well-worn copy of Dr. Spock's *Baby and Child Care* rested on my bedside table. As I scanned the book's pages about head injuries, her cries seemed to subside. According to Dr. Spock, she was showing no symptoms of having suffered anything serious. I sponged her forehead with a cool washcloth and then held her on my lap, murmuring words of love. Minutes later she was all smiles, playing with the cat as though nothing had happened.

But I was still shaken.

Oh, God, I thought, *I feel my daughter's pain so deeply. Is it possible that this is how You love me, too?*

It was a brilliant summer day, and little nuisances had stolen the morning. Within the hour, Tom was expecting us to meet him for lunch at his office in downtown Minneapolis. But I was still in my nightgown. And so was Katy. Seated in her high chair, she had more egg in her hair and on her cheeks than in her tummy, and she was blissfully oblivious to our need to hurry.

Across the room, the television was tuned to *Sesame Street*. A big blue letter K danced across the screen. Katy caught sight of it and threw her hands skyward—inadvertently launching a full mug of milk across the dining room.

"*Katy!*"

I was about to scold when I caught myself. In recent days, I'd noticed how sensitive my daughter seemed to my moods and reprimands, especially when my tone was harsh.

She regarded me warily.

"Katy," I repeated calmly, bending over to pick up the empty mug. "Do you know what you say when you spill your milk?" I touched her tousled head and smiled. "You say, '*Oops!*'"

A big, sunny grin lit her face, and I wiped up the floor, feeling so grateful for not giving in to irritation.

Thank You, God, I thought. *You are forever patient. Even in my worst moments, You still love me. You always offer forgiveness.*

I looked in wonder at the little figure in the high chair—my daughter. Although she couldn't know it, she was creating a new love in me—mother love. Fresh from heaven, she was also surprising me with glimpses of God's love—the perfect love of my heavenly Father, eternally caring, patient, and forgiving.

Thank You, God, for my daughter!

Moving Day

It was moving day—a late summer afternoon in the green and pleasant suburb of Minnetonka, Minnesota.

Our little house on Creek View Trail was now empty. All traces of our family's presence had been removed by an efficient army of impersonal moving men. At the time we decided to move to New York, I knew that leaving Minnesota wouldn't be easy. Moving never is. At best it is stressful, disruptive, and expensive. For me, however, the hardest part was saying good-bye to our good neighbors and our friends from church, plus saying good-bye to what had been our first home—the site for so many good and happy memories.

Now, I took one last walk through the empty rooms. As I paused in the doorway of our baby Katy's nursery, my eyes traveled to a spot above her window. There, on her Disney wallpaper, Dumbo's trunk appeared where Tinkerbell's wand rightfully belonged, and Snow White was surrounded by five and one-half dwarfs instead of seven.

Just days before Katy's birth, my husband, Tom, and I had impulsively decided to paper the tiny room; many times since, we had laughed, remembering how the salesclerk had assured us that the job would take "a few hours." Not only had we worked for an entire weekend, but we'd run half a roll short of paper! Hence our crazy patch.

With those memories, it finally hit me: we were moving. A bittersweet ache filled my heart. Still standing there, I felt Tom quietly come up beside me. His eyes followed mine to the wallpaper patch above

Katy's window. As though reading my thoughts, his hand reached out to hold mine tightly.

"Don't worry, Kitty," he whispered. "We're taking the love in this room with us."

Suddenly, in a very real way, I sensed that God, too, was with us in that empty little room with the patched wallpaper. I knew that no matter how far away we moved, or how many more times, God would always be with us—guiding us, protecting us, and touching our lives. It was God's love, after all, that had made our house in Minnesota a home, and it was God's love that would surely do the same for the two-bedroom apartment waiting for us in New York.

Didn't the apostle Paul tell us in Romans that absolutely nothing can separate God's children from His love? "Neither death, nor life, nor angels, nor principalities, nor powers, nor things present, nor things to come …" (Romans 8:38–39).

I knew that this was so. Nothing—not even life in big and bustling New York City—could separate us from God.

And thanks to God's loving presence, New York, like Minnetonka, indeed became our home.

City Sunset

One muggy summer evening in New York City, my sister, Laurrie, and I were bicycling along the Hudson River when she suggested we stop at one of the piers to watch the sunset.

"What?" I asked. "Look at a sunset from here?"

The pier seemed an unlikely spot from which to view anything. Abandoned and littered, jutting out into the murky waters of the Hudson, it pointed west toward the smokestacks of the New Jersey shoreline.

"Come on," my sister called. "Follow me!"

We pedaled onto the blacktopped pier, where a small crowd had gathered. Some sat quietly on old pilings. Others ventured to the river's edge, finding places on the broken concrete breakwater. We were all looking to the west, waiting.

Soundlessly, the great red sun edged its way toward the horizon, bathing land and sky in rose-colored light. Spellbound, we watched in silence as the sun sank behind the skyline of the distant shore until only a thin crescent remained. Finally that too disappeared.

Not one of us on that pier moved. Not a word was said. For a moment, we remained in the thrall of something so pure, so majestic that it could only come from God.

And then, as one, we burst into spontaneous applause.

Little Katy

Katy's Kingdom

There is a wonderful legend in Judaism that says that while a child is in the womb, she learns all about God and His heavenly kingdom, and then—just before the child is born—an angel descends and taps his finger on her lips and says, "Hush, don't tell anyone what you know." This, so the legend goes, is why we are born with a dimple above our lips and, more importantly, why we remember so little of our spiritual origins. It is an attempt to explain our instinctive sense that children do, indeed, arrive in this world fresh from heaven. Close to God, they come to us bringing messages of faith, hope, and—if we look closely—glimpses of our Creator's loving nature and kingdom.

In academic circles, some theorize that newborns are actually more in touch with the world of the spirit than adults. That is, from the moment of conception and throughout the months before birth, they enjoy intimate communion with their Creator. In this view, the concrete world into which we are born is a new reality we must learn to comprehend. Through the five senses, we gradually understand patterns of sunlight on the nursery wall, the gaily colored mobile hanging above the crib, and Mommy's and Daddy's smiling faces. Over time, so the theory goes, we *unlearn* the world of the spirit, which, prompted by a disquieting sense of "something missing," we can spend much of our adult life trying to recapture.

When our daughter Katy was born, I often wondered if she might have access to some sort of special world that only she could see. Many times I observed her staring with keen interest at what appeared to me to be nothing more than the air above her white Jenny Lind crib. As she stared, entranced, a flicker of what I could only call recognition lit her gray-blue eyes. Inexplicably, she gurgled and laughed, as though witness to some delightful scene.

What did Katy see?

Perhaps nothing. Then again …

As though brushed by the gossamer tip of a passing angel's wings, I shivered with wonder at the possibilities. Over time, I came to believe that she did possess some sort of transcendent vision into another world—"Katy's Kingdom," I came to think of it.

As months passed and Katy began to take her first steps, it seemed she no longer had time to spend gazing into space. She was too busy learning about the concrete world around her. She took particular delight in identifying simple, everyday objects—cat, spoon, book, apple.

One day, while I was sorting through a stack of old magazines that had accumulated by the side of my bed, Katy toddled into the room. Running to my side, she reached for an issue that, to my dismay, featured on its cover a depressing photo of a street person dressed in tattered rags.

"Read!" said Katy, clutching the magazine in her chubby fist and plopping down, cross-legged, on the floor.

"No-no, honey," I said gently.

Not wanting her to see the distressing photo, I reached to remove the magazine. I was stopped by Katy's delighted cry as she pointed to the picture and identified—with the absolute joy that is the exclusive property of two-year-olds—"Mommy, look! Apple!"

Sure enough, there clutched in the street person's gnarled, dirty hand was a luscious red apple. Again I was reminded of Katy's Kingdom— her uncanny ability to perceive the beautiful and the extraordinary in the most ordinary situations. On the one hand, considering Katy's innocence and naiveté, it was really quite *unremarkable* that she should find something lovely in what for me was an altogether homely scene. On the other hand …

Sitting down on the floor next to Katy, I wrapped my arms around her and pulled her close.

Why, I wondered, *did I not even notice the apple?*

A few months later, Katy and I were walking home from our neighborhood grocery store. While I maneuvered her stroller, heavy-laden with parcels, along the cracked city sidewalk, Katy scampered alongside me. Whenever Katy and I walked home in this manner, I marveled at how different our objectives were. My goal was to get home—fast. For Katy, however, each stroll was an open-ended adventure.

Now, dashing ahead, she stopped briefly to hug her favorite pillow-shaped potted shrub.

"Oo-o-h," she squealed, wrinkling her tiny nose against the shrub's sharp needles. "Prickles!"

Then, bending to pick up a pebble, she ran to a nearby grate in the sidewalk.

"Look!" she cried, dropping the pebble through the grate and watching in wonder as it fell into the darkness below.

Our next stop was the *New York Times* newspaper dispenser on the corner or, more precisely, the shiny black button on the dispenser, which Katy liked to push. En route to the button, however, Katy froze, transfixed.

"Look, Mommy!" she cried. *"Water!"*

I followed her gaze to the bright red fire hydrant five yards ahead. The cap was off, and a steady stream of water splashed to the curb and ran down Greenwich Street as far as the eye could see. For the next few minutes, I knelt and joined Katy as she examined the flow of water with its myriad crystalline reflections—sky, clouds, buildings—all swirling around as though viewed through fun-house mirrors. Together we felt the coolness of the water on our hands and listened to the gentle splash it made as it hit the pavement and trickled on down the street, carrying with it fragile boats of fallen twigs and ginkgo leaves.

Had I been walking alone, I would never have given the fire hydrant a second look. Once more I had been privileged to enter Katy's Kingdom; I had been allowed to share her ability to transcend the commonplace and see *something more*.

At that moment, I was struck by the similarity between Katy's Kingdom and the kingdom of God described in the Bible. Just as through the eyes of my child I was enabled to see something more, likewise through the eyes of faith, I was enabled to see the something more of God's invisible kingdom: hope in despair, healing in illness, peace in turmoil, even life in death. Jesus said, "Truly I tell you, unless you change and become like little children, you will never enter the kingdom of heaven" (Matthew 18:3, KJV).

As Katy and I rounded the corner and headed down Horatio Street toward home, I thanked God for sending me this little ambassador, through whose eyes I was learning to glimpse His kingdom more clearly.

Family Forever!

When I got married, there was a lot of pressure for modern working women to keep their maiden names. But I eagerly gave mine up. This was because *Brinckerhoff* was so often mispronounced and difficult to spell—especially with that tricky little *c* tucked away in the middle. How many times as a kid I longed to be a Smith or a Jones!

So what did I go and do? As though bewitched by some mischievous ancestor, I passed the name on to our son.

"Brink?" people asked with an all-too-familiar tone of puzzlement upon first encountering our towheaded boy.

"Brinck," I confirmed, not even beginning to try and explain the spelling. "*John Brinckerhoff*, actually." I stopped. "It's—you know—a family name."

In the weeks preceding Brinck's first birthday, our mailbox became increasingly crowded with enthusiastic letters and notes from a variety of distant, never-met relations.

"Greetings," they wrote, "to members of the Brin(c)kerhoff[1] Family by name or blood everywhere! On Saturday, August 24, 1985, there's going to be a family reunion in Ridgefield Park, New Jersey." Apparently Ridgefield Park was a Brinkerhoff stronghold, and the site for the last Brin(c)kerhoff Reunion—one hundred years earlier, in the summer of 1885.

Initially I felt reluctant about accepting the invitation. I'd always regarded family reunions (along with family coats-of-arms and genealogies) with something of a raised eyebrow—at worst, pretentious;

---

1 There are two spellings of Brin(c)kerhoff in America—one with and one without the *c*. In Holland today, the name is spelled Brinkerhof.

My wonderful dad, John "Brinck" Brinckerhoff

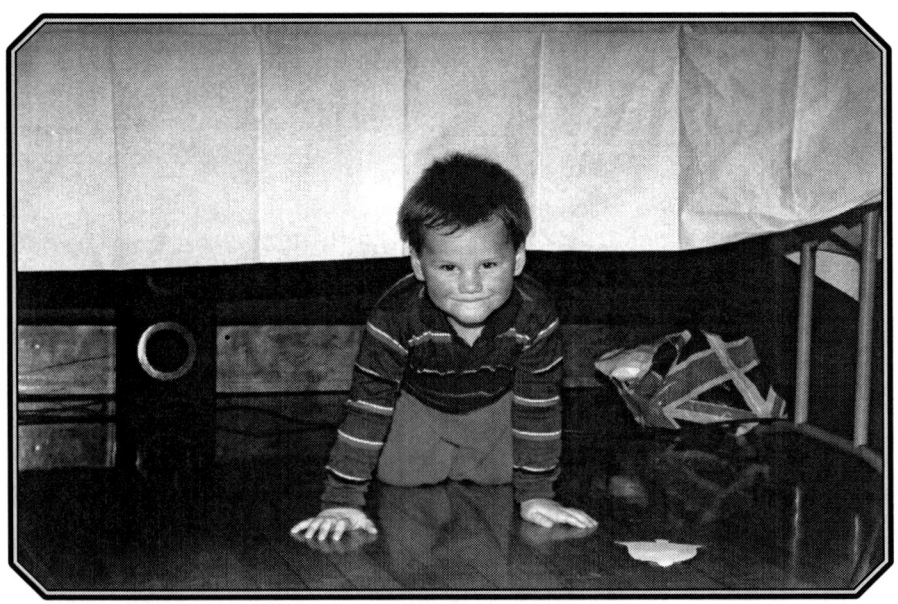

Little Brinck

at best, well, a little old-fashioned. But the true source of my hesitation was something else. Though it had been five years since my father's death, there was a still-hurting part of me that had not yet fully resolved his passing. As my children were born, it grieved me to think that neither Katy nor Brinck would ever know their grandfather, and worse, to think that Dad would never know *them*: Katy, so like him, full of kindness and compassion, and Brinck, to his namesake true, ever-bubbling with fun and sunny *joie de vivre*. No, to attend the reunion—my father's reunion—would surely bring back painful feelings I'd rather let alone.

Still, as weeks passed and letters from Ridgefield Park kept coming, the enthusiasm of the reunion organizers proved contagious.

And so it was that early on a hot and muggy Saturday, six of us—Tom, Katy, Brinck, my sister, Laurrie, my mother, and I—all left our Greenwich Village apartments and headed north on Manhattan's Westside Highway.

There we were, traveling up alongside the Hudson River in New York, the city that was once *Nieuw Amsterdam*, the very place that our first American ancestor, Joris Dircksen Brinckerhoff, had landed when he stepped off the good ship *Den Eyckenboom* (*The Oak Tree*) in 1641. Moving through the Lincoln Tunnel, we found ourselves sharing the bits and pieces of history we knew about our family ... how Joris was the first and only elected elder of Brooklyn's Old Dutch Church and how as *zieken-trooster*, or "comforter of the sick," he was required to visit the sick every day and read aloud from the Bible ... how Joris's youngest boy, Dirck, was killed by Indians on Staten Island ... how fond George Washington was of old Colonel John Brinckerhoff, and how Washington stayed often in the spare bedroom behind the parlor in the colonel's old homestead in Fishkill.

We talked about the tiny hamlet of Brinckerhoff, New York ... Brinkerhoff barbed wire ... Brinkerhoff pianos ... the Brinckerhoff engineer who invented the third-rail system of subway transportation ... our great-grandfather Gilbert Brinckerhoff, a sort of turn-of-the-century Indiana Jones explorer and photojournalist. We chatted about all manner of Brinckerhoffs, famous and infamous, with and without the *c*, living and long departed.

All but one.

If only Dad could be with us ...

In the town center of Ridgefield Park, a parade was just beginning. Bedecked in Colonial-style costumes and marching to the steady beat of the high school band and local bagpipe corps, many family members sported banners identifying the states from which they hailed: New Jersey, California, Montana, Indiana, Ohio, Mississippi—maybe forty states; I lost count.

After years of being if not the only, then one of the very few, Brinckerhoffs in the phone book, how wonderfully strange it was to find myself smiling and nodding to so many fellow Brin(c)kerhoffs. We checked each others' name tags and introduced ourselves and our children. No name was mispronounced on this day. And how good it was to meet so many "Brincks"! I counted five—and there were probably more.

One hundred years before at precisely this same spot, the Brin(c)kerhoffs celebrated their bicentennial reunion with lectures on family history, singing, praying, dancing, eating ice cream, and assembling for group photographs. In many ways, our reunion was much the same.

Following a buffet luncheon in the high school cafeteria, we moved to the auditorium, where the special guest was one Frits Brinkerhof, a student from Roermond, Holland. The genuine article!

According to Frits, there were about twenty-five Brinkerhof families living in Holland today, compared with the hundreds of families here in America. Suddenly I saw our clan for what it really was—a microcosm of America, the Melting Pot. Though our name might be Dutch, we had, over the past three centuries, become English, Irish, French, Italian, Hungarian, German, Polish, Austrian, Swedish, and more. And it was the same with our vocations. Joris Dircksen and his sons had been farmers. There were present-day Brin(c)kerhoff farmers among us this day, as well as stockbrokers, airline pilots, social workers, artists, authors, mailmen, doctors, builders, botanists, mothers (lots of these!), and—Joris would have been pleased—a fair share of ministers.

As I sat in the cool auditorium surrounded by some 250 kin, it occurred to me that had I encountered any of these people on the street just hours before, I would have passed them without a glance, dismissing them as strangers. But here we were, inextricably linked by name and blood, wondrously united, if only for a few fleeting hours, in time and space. How, after this, could I ever so easily dismiss *anyone* as a stranger again? Weren't we all, ultimately, part of an even larger family—the family of humankind—bonded by our common Creator Father? Like so many people in our fast-paced, fragmented world, I had moved a lot and called—but not truly considered—a lot of places home. To experience such a powerful sense of connectedness, of continuity, felt—well, good. Very good indeed.

Too soon the reunion was over. Somehow, after such an exhilarating day, it just didn't seem appropriate to plunge ourselves into the dreary Lincoln Tunnel, so Tom volunteered to take us home via the bridge named for Colonel Brinckerhoff's friend, George Washington.

Looming before us was the bridge's magnificent network of cables, now liquid gold in the late-afternoon sun. Brinck's slumbering head rested heavily, like a piece of ripe fruit, on my shoulder. Katy, too, was dreaming, her summer-browned legs stretched out across two laps, the fingers of her left hand half-curled around her brother's chubby fist.

It was my sister who broke the silence.

"Remember the day," asked Laurrie gently, "when Daddy came home with that trout from Miss Jewel's pond?"

To my surprise, the question did not, as it would have just a few hours earlier, cause me to feel a pang of grief. Yes, I remembered. And with the memory, I smiled.

At that moment I knew—I knew without a doubt—that somehow, in the mystery of God's loving kindness, my father's paradise included the knowing and loving of his grandchildren. With the same certainty, I also knew that they, beginning this day, would come to know and love their grandfather.

How?

They would know him through the memories we shared, through the stories we told, through scrapbooks and photographs and old home movies. They would come to know and love him through those of us who already did—through their family. For a family we were, each of us part of that divinely sanctioned whole through which God's grace, like a golden thread, promised to bind us powerfully together—across the miles, over the years …

Forever.

Mirror, Mirror

As I hung up the telephone, I caught a glimpse of my face in the hall mirror. It was an unhappy face, with a pinched brow and a curled-down mouth. A face twisted with envy.

A friend had phoned to tell me about her husband's big promotion. Now, she said, they would be able to buy their dream home—a spectacular penthouse apartment overlooking one of Manhattan's most beautiful parks. I could still hear my voice feigning happiness for her good fortune while all the time I was burning with envy.

Why, I wondered, *do I feel that her gain is somehow my loss?*

I sat for a full minute by the phone, stewing, when I became aware of a colorful sparkle of light on the wall across from me—a prism reflected from the beveled edge of the mirror in which I'd just viewed my unhappy face. That old mirror. The mirror I'd paid fifteen dollars for at a Florida flea market. I'd just graduated from college and was struggling to furnish my first apartment. With its ornately carved turn-of-the-century oval frame, how pretty the mirror had seemed at the time. A real find. But now it just seemed commonplace and old.

I never thought I was the type of person who would get caught "keeping up with the Joneses." I'd never thought of myself as competitive. But somehow with the passing years, I'd developed a nasty jealous streak. I knew this was wrong thinking, and yet it just seemed that so many people I knew had so much *more*. Charming brownstone houses with sunny gardens. Co-ops and condos with landscaped terraces. Country houses in the Hamptons, in the Berkshires, and atop snowcapped mountains in Vermont. Why, I'd never even heard of a "country house" before moving to New York. It would be easy to blame my jealousy on the city. After all, it was harder to imagine a more competitive or materialistic place. But I knew in my heart the problem wasn't my location. It was me. Jealousy, that old green-eyed monster, had the ability to swoop in and attack at any given moment, darkening the brightest day. Truly, its power was frightening.

I glanced again at my face reflected in the mirror. Yep, it was unhappy all right. A sour puss if there ever was one. If only I could somehow find the power to change.

My thoughts were interrupted by the sound of Katy calling.

"Mommy!"

Just turned four, Katy barreled down the hall clutching the game *Candy Land* under her arm. It was a birthday gift from my mother, Katy's first board game ever, and she wanted to play.

"Not now," I said, preferring instead to nurse my miserable state of discontent.

"Please?"

Sighing, I followed Katy into the room, and we sat cross-legged on the hardwood floor. Katy set up the game between us: a stack of color-coded cards and a number of playing pieces that looked like tiny plastic gingerbread men. The cards we selected would advance us to the game's ultimate goal: arrival at the Candy Castle.

I picked a green man for luck—or maybe envy. Katy picked red, her favorite color. Being the birthday girl, she went first and picked a card illustrated with a purple sugarplum, which sent her nine spaces down the board.

Soon I took a strong lead via Gumdrop Pass, while Katy, to my dismay, got stuck in Molasses Swamp. This was not good. The last thing I wanted to do was win. For me to win, I reasoned, meant that Katy would lose. And that, I was quite certain, would break her heart. So I tried to let Katy get ahead by "forgetting" to advance my playing piece.

But Katy caught on.

"Mommy," she chided, her little brow furrowed with concern. "You forgot to move your man. You've got to move so you can get to the Candy Castle."

Too soon, the game was over. Despite my best efforts to hold him back, my tiny green man arrived at the Candy Castle. Before I could say I was sorry, Katy cried out.

"Oh, Mommy!" she exclaimed, clapping her little hands ecstatically. "You did it! You got to the Candy Castle!" She wasn't dismayed at all. She was happy for me.

Lunging across the game board, she threw her arms around my neck. I laughed and tickled her behind her knees. The two of us collapsed, a tangle of arms and legs and giggles and glee. In the midst of the merriment, Katy's words, like distant wind chimes, sang in my mind …

"You did it," she had said. Not, "You won."

In the most astonishing way, at this point in her young life, Katy had absolutely no concept of winning—or losing. Her instinctive response to my good fortune was not envy or disappointment or a sense of loss. It was joy—sheer joy.

And why not?

I looked at my daughter in amazement. Here was a child so pure, so untarnished, so fresh from God that she had not yet learned about the darker sides of human nature. Was I so far from God myself? Was I so hardened by life that I couldn't be happy for others? Oh God, I hoped not.

Shame on me, I thought. *Just looking at Katy, how dare I want for anything? God has blessed me so abundantly. He has given me a loving husband and two healthy children … a comfortable apartment on a peaceful treelined street … good food on our table … family, friends, and a wonderful church close by.*

I started for the telephone to call my friend to let her know how *really* happy I was for her when …

"Look!" Katy grabbed my hand and pulled toward her open bedroom door and the hallway beyond.

"Look, Mommy," she repeated. "Rainbows!"

There, dancing on the wall, were half a dozen brilliantly hued shimmers of light from the old mirror across the hall. I touched the mirror gently, causing the rainbows to dance, and Katy's eyes opened wide.

The face in the mirror, I noticed, was not so unhappy now. The features seemed somehow softer, more relaxed. And the corners of the mouth were slightly upturned. Hold on. Was that a smile I saw?

Again I touched the mirror, admiring its fine workmanship, marveling at its survival over so many years.

You handsome old thing. I grinned. *What a find.*

The Broken Vase

Early one Saturday morning, I was rudely awakened by a loud crash in the living room.

"The cat!" I cried to Tom, who was already out of bed and halfway to the scene of the crime. "Nicholas knocked something over!" Sadly, our beloved calico cat Indy had passed away, but Santa had brought our family Nicholas, a slate-gray scamp with a snowy-white nose. Unlike his placid predecessor, Nicholas was adventuresome, rambunctious—and a little bit clumsy.

Like a bank security camera, my mind's eye scanned the contents of the living room for potential disaster areas while I waited for Tom to report the damage. The crash had been loud—too loud to have been caused by any of my numerous china and glass knickknacks.

Then I remembered the vase. The beautiful antique Chinese vase on the table at the far end of the room. The vase that held a lush, colorful arrangement of silk flowers that Nicholas loved to nibble. Tom had surprised me with it on our fifth anniversary.

"It's the vase," Tom confirmed, returning to the room and crawling back in bed as though nothing had happened.

"Did it break?" I knew it was a silly question, but one could always hope.

Tom nodded.

"That dumb cat!" I exploded. And then, to my great embarrassment, I burst into tears. *Get a grip*, I scolded myself. *After all, it's just a vase.* You'd think by now, after living with two small children and as many curious cats, I would be used to things breaking. "Oh, Tom," I sniffed, "you know how much I loved that vase. Do you think we could get another one?"

"I don't think so," he replied. "We're operating on a pretty tight budget."

"But it was so beautiful!"

"Maybe you can fix it," he said.

"Fix it?" I cried, reaching for a tissue and blowing my nose. "You've got to be kidding. And even if I could, it would be worthless. That's the way it is with antiques. One chip, one crack, and they're worthless."

"This is no way to start a weekend," Tom said, pulling the blanket up over his ears. "The kids will be up soon. Try to get some sleep."

I pulled on my robe and padded out to the darkened living room to view the wreckage for myself. It was worse than I had imagined. Turning on the light, I knelt and began to sort the pieces—about six large fragments, a dozen or so smaller ones, and countless slivers and chips of ceramic glaze.

Fix it?

There was nothing for me to do now but sweep up the mess and throw it out.

"That darn cat," I muttered under my breath, bending under the table where the vase had stood to reach for the last fragment. As I placed it next to the others, I couldn't help but admire how beautiful it was, with its delicately hued pattern of Oriental birds, fruits, and flowers. Suddenly, like a child drawn to the magic of a jigsaw puzzle, I found myself gently aligning the broken fragment with another that looked as if it might match. I was amazed at how clean the break had been, how surprisingly seamless the two pieces looked when I pushed them together.

Fix it?

Somehow the task no longer seemed quite so hopeless. I tiptoed into Katy and Brinck's bedroom and rummaged through their box of art supplies until I found what I was looking for—the trusty white bottle of Elmer's Glue-All with the bright orange cap.

Throughout the morning and for the remainder of the day, I sat on the floor where the vase had broken, absorbed in the painstaking process of matching and gluing the broken pieces together. Even Katy and Brinck helped, dividing their time between shooing away the ever-curious Nicholas and counting the seconds as best they could ("... ten, eleven-teen, thirteen, twenty-teen ...") while we waited for the glue to dry.

By suppertime, the job was done. From just a few feet away, Tom commented that he couldn't even tell the vase had been broken.

I was elated.

As I set the vase back on the table, turning it just so with its best side facing forward, I felt not only a deep personal satisfaction for the job I had done, but a strange sort of kinship with this survivor. True, the vase was now chipped and cracked—but *worthless?* Hardly. In fact, it seemed more beautiful than I remembered it.

In this broken but repaired vessel, I saw reflected what God's love had done for me when I—broken, chipped, and flawed—had fallen and crashed. From the day I first heard the good news of God's love and believed, my heavenly Father had picked me up, pieced me together, and ever-so-gently made me whole. Not all at once, but piece by piece.

He was doing it still.

How to Recharge Your Churchgoing

A little while after the arrival of our second child, something happened to my churchgoing. Sunday mornings became a mad rush to get the four of us fed, dressed, and out the door. After depositing Katy and Brinck in the church nursery, I was often late and would end up guiltily slinking down the aisle and sliding into the pew next to Tom in the middle of a hymn. Or prayer. Or during the announcements. During the sermon, my mind wandered. The liturgy and prayers became numbingly familiar. Bored and restless, I grew critical of the sermon and the choir. Sometimes nothing—not even Communion—stirred my heart.

What had happened with my desire and ability to worship? I felt tense, frustrated, and guilty. It wasn't just the added responsibilities of being both mother and wife; I had plenty of help from Tom on Sunday mornings. No, there was something amiss with my attitude. Church had become like a marriage with no romance—all duty and obligation, no surprises. No joy.

One Sunday morning I found myself asking God for help (something I should have done from the start!), and it occurred to me that my problem was, indeed, just like rekindling romance in marriage. After all, it was my *relationship* with God that had gone stale. I talked to my pastor, I talked to friends, I talked to Tom, and this is what I decided to do about rejuvenating Sundays in church.

One: Go to church with a sense of anticipation.

In one article I read, a minister wrote, "If you sit in the pew expecting nothing, nothing is what you'll get." God is like the father of the prodigal, who, when he saw his son a long way off, rushed to welcome him home. When you go to church, think about how exciting it is that God is there waiting eagerly for you with outstretched arms. He loves you *so* much!

Two: Get there early.

If you're like me, this means setting my alarm and getting up earlier in the morning. Arriving at church a few minutes early lets you prepare for worship in a relaxed fashion as you think about the upcoming service. It's a good time to bring God your personal list of thanksgivings, petitions, and prayer requests. There have been times when I actually carried along a written list to help me focus my thoughts.

Three: Pray for those around you.

Take a look around and say a silent prayer for family, friends, ushers, choir members, and strangers. One woman I know always looks for someone in the congregation whose shoulders are drooping or who seems a bit sad. And don't forget the clergy! Often our ministers are bearing the burdens of many in the congregation, as well as their own.

Four: Look for God in unexpected places.

God can reveal Himself in the Scriptures, the sermon, the hymns, the prayers, and even in the building itself. One Sunday I found myself gazing at a carved wooden angel in front of the choir stalls. It made me think of the wonder of angels in general, and of the person who carved that angel so many years ago, and of how that sculptor and I were connected in Christ.

Five: Study up.

As my minister reminded me, church on Sundays only is not necessarily enough for a person's continuing spiritual growth. A midweek Bible study or healing service, a prayer group, a regular time of private devotions—all of these can further enhance the worship experience. I have a good friend—an older woman I think of as a spiritual dynamo—who finds out ahead of time what the Scripture passage will be for each Sunday so she will get more out of its reading!

"Let me tell you a little secret," this same wise woman said. "Expect something exciting to happen to your spiritual life every Sunday. If you believe it will happen and pray for it to happen, it *will* happen. That's a promise that was once made to me, and so far it's never failed."

Liberty Weekend

"Mommy! Come quick!"

I hurried into Katy's bedroom, where I found her kneeling on her window seat, her small freckled nose pressed against the glass. Just turned five, she gazed wide-eyed as three mammoth blimps moved noiselessly across Manhattan's southern skyline.

I wrapped my arms around her waist, and the two of us watched as one by one the blimps disappeared behind the twin towers of the World Trade Center and then reappeared on the other side, moving on in their lumbering yet graceful fashion.

"Miss Liberty's having a birthday! Miss Liberty's having a birthday!" sang Katy.

Our time together—as so often seemed the case these days—was too soon over. Katy wriggled from my grasp and danced into the living room for a better view.

It was early morning on July 3, 1986, and yes, the Statue of Liberty, that grand old lady of New York, was one day away from marking her one hundredth anniversary—a celebration that promised to be the most extravagant in the city's, if not the nation's, history.

We, however, would not be there.

Having long ago decided to avoid the crowds and commotion of Liberty Weekend in the city, Tom and I had opted instead for a low-key family holiday in the colorful village of Montauk, New York, on the tip of Long Island, some 120 miles—and worlds—away.

Brinck and Katy, Montauk, New York

The sun was now high and hot on the back of my neck as I buckled two-year-old Brinck into his car seat. I tossed Katy her Mickey Mouse pillow and journey's supply of picture books and crayons. Tom slammed the packed trunk shut. I opened the front passenger door, about to get in the car, when for some inexplicable reason I looked up.

The blimps were back, this time accompanied by half a dozen helicopters buzzing importantly in the cloudless sky. There was an air of anticipation in the city. American flags fluttered restlessly from apartment and storefront windows. In the distance, I glimpsed the graceful outline of a tall ship, majestic and proud, making its way south along the Hudson River.

And suddenly, more than anything in the world, New York City, *not* Montauk, Long Island, was where I wanted to be.

But Tom turned the key in the ignition, and we pulled away from our apartment building on Horatio Street and headed east, through the Queens Midtown Tunnel, and onto the Long Island Expressway. And the farther we traveled from home, the more my yearning to return to the city swelled.

Never mind that once we arrived in Montauk, Katy, Brinck, and Tom had the time of their lives. The surf, high and powerful, elicited delicious squeals of excitement from the children. In the late afternoon, we biked to the marina, where we watched fishermen unload their day's catch of yellowfin tuna, porgies, sharks, and lobsters. Dinner was alfresco: fried clams, slaw, and hot buttered corn on the cob at Gossman's Dock, where Katy and Brinck gleefully hurled their French fries at fat white gulls that snatched the morsels in midair. Never mind that Tom was more relaxed and rested than I could remember seeing him in months. Never mind all these things.

I wanted to be home in the city.

And why not? I sulked. Even in Montauk, it seemed I was surrounded by newspapers, radios, and televisions, all proclaiming the glories of Liberty Weekend in New York City, that once-in-a-lifetime experience for those charmed souls so lucky to be there.

By the evening of the Fourth, I had managed to work myself into a funk of major proportions.

"Move it!" I barked at Katy and Brinck as we scrambled over the dunes toward the beach for the town's nine-o'clock display of fireworks. Even in July, the night air was cool and blustery. Jammies and sneakers peeked out from beneath the children's tightly zipped parkas.

But here in Montauk, there was no need to hurry. The crowd was sparse, maybe one hundred townspeople and tourists scattered along the football field-sized stretch of darkened beach. Here and there, clusters of youngsters were illuminated by the flicker of handheld sparklers, and the rhythm of the surf was punctuated by the occasional blaze and whine of a Roman candle.

We spread our blanket on the sand and huddled close. Tom held Brinck in his lap, and Katy nestled cozily in the hammock of my crossed legs.

"Back home, people are watching the biggest pyrotechnic display in history," I grumbled to no one in particular. "Forty-one thousand fireworks shot from forty-one barges in computerized perfection."

The wind off the Atlantic was strong, and the fireworks in Montauk had a difficult time staying airborne. Some exploded in a modest display of color and light. Others fizzled or were swiftly blown away like dandelion puffs.

There was a pause in the proceedings.

"Think that last firework was the grand finale?" I asked Tom.

"I don't know," he replied. "Don't folks usually applaud when the show's over?"

Another firework.

Another pause.

"Maybe *that* was the grand finale?" Despite my gloominess, a smile began to tug at the corners of my mouth.

As though sensing my brightening mood, Katy glanced up at me and snuggled closer, and it occurred to me that since our arrival at the beach, I'd been holding my daughter for the longest single uninterrupted stretch of time in months—maybe a year. No longer plump and soft like her baby brother, Katy's body had grown surprisingly lean and strong. *When had this happened?* A bittersweet ache grabbed at my heart.

How fast you are growing, my little Katy! If only I could hold onto you—to this moment—forever!

Suddenly I no longer wanted to be watching the great extravaganza in New York City. I wanted nothing more than to be here on the beach at Montauk, holding my daughter close.

The wind off the ocean died down, and the black night sky exploded in a noble grand finale of silver and gold. The sound of applause drifted up and down the beach.

Thank You, God, I thought as we shook the sand from our blanket and headed back to the car. *Thank You for this special night in this special place. Even when I find myself where I think I don't want to be, You are always there, transforming the situation with Your grace—surprising me with Your presence.*

Summertime Fun

Ah, Summertime

Ah, summertime.

It's a warm, breezy Sunday evening, and I open the sliding screen door and step out onto the deck of our beach house for a deep breath of fresh ocean air.

My two children, golden brown from their days in the summer sun, are now sleeping soundly, serenaded by a chorus of crickets. Tom has taken the train back to the city for another week at work. I'm alone on the upper deck of this saltbox house in an old fishing village on the far eastern tip of Long Island.

The sound of distant laughter floats on the night air. I glance across the yard to our neighbors' homes, lit from within by a warm, cozy glow. The families inside are together, playing games and carrying on. The only light coming from our windows behind me is the cold blue flicker of the television set I'd turned on for company.

In the east the sky is briefly lit by the rhythmic sweep of light coming from the two-hundred-year-old lighthouse at Montauk Point. In the searchlight's wake, thousands of stars twinkle in astonishing hues of rose, emerald, and azure. I catch my breath. Some are like gemstones piercing the night sharply; the Milky Way glows fuzzily, a chiffon scarf strewn across the heavens.

How long has it been since I've seen stars like this? In the wintertime, housebound in the city, I find there's not much chance for stargazing. But a July night like this is meant for it. I wonder how many other people are doing just what I am doing now. It doesn't matter where they are at this moment—standing in tiny backyards, sitting on city stoops, lying in sleeping bags in forest clearings—the stars belong to them too. We share them.

The ringing of the telephone calls me back into the house. I slide the screen door shut and turn off the television. It's Tom on the phone. It's good to hear his voice, but somehow I no longer feel quite so alone, not on a night like this, not on a night when the heavens are so wondrously declaring His glory.

Ah, summertime.

Katy at Gossman's Dock, Montauk, New York

Chicken Pox!

Crisp air, cloudless blue sky. It is an absolutely glorious spring day in New York City—and for the children and me, it's our first outing in more than a week since a tiny pink spot behind Katy's left ear marked the arrival of a most unwelcome visitor—chicken pox.

It is late morning, nearing noon, and Abingdon Square Park is empty, save for a flock of hungry pigeons at the black iron gate.

How busy those birds are! Heads down, beaks pressed close to the asphalt, they pick and peck and scrape at the remains of someone's breakfast-on-the-go—a bagel and cream cheese purchased at the Korean deli across the street, then hurriedly tossed to the pavement with the lumbering arrival of the Number 10 bus.

I roll the stroller over to a park bench beneath a cluster of trees, their spindly branches dotted with fat buds. Soon they will be offering shade from a hot summer sun. The green paint on the bench is blistered and flaking from winter's cold rains and snow. I find my seat, and then, to my right, I spread a paper napkin on the bench and begin to set out the children's lunch: PB & J's on whole wheat bread, red seedless grapes, carrot sticks, brownies, and apple juice in two brick cardboard cartons that come with their own cellophane-wrapped mini-straws.

Thank the Lord, little Katy's finally on the mend, I think. *She's doing just fine.* All that's left of her bout with "the pox" is a smattering of spots on her tummy and back, now concealed by clothing. I watch as she swings her limber five (going on six)-year-old body up, over, and around the highest bar on the rainbow-shaped jungle gym. Her two-year-old brother follows, clambering like a little blonde chimp up the weather-beaten apparatus.

The happy moment is suddenly darkened by a worrisome cloud of a thought.

True, Katy's doing fine. But what about Brinck?

According to the pediatrician, because Brinck has been exposed to the chicken pox virus, three more weeks will have to pass before we will find out whether he, too, is going to get the pox. *Three long weeks* during which, because he is potentially contagious, I will have to do my best to keep him away from other children.

Will Brinck get the pox? Won't he get the pox? Poor little guy. More to the point, poor *me!*

One would think that in this scientific and technologically advanced age of antibiotics, computers, and space shuttles, someone, somewhere, would have discovered a vaccine for a malady so homely, so miserable, so old-fashioned—okay, let's face it—so downright *inconvenient* as the chicken pox![2]

All too soon our pleasant outing will be over, and I wince at the thought of the apartment that awaits our return—rooms cluttered with cotton balls and putty-colored calamine lotion, piles of coloring books and dried-out magic markers, hundreds of snips and scraps of leftover construction paper, and nearly as many bits and pieces of dried-up Play-Doh.

Chicken pox!

Why, when we're housebound, does it seem that television has nothing to offer but boring soap operas and even duller game shows? And I'd sure like to have a few words with the person who wrote the book *Fun & Easy Things to Do with Stuff around the House.*

"But, honey," I tried to explain to my crestfallen, itchy, highly contagious daughter at the height of her illness, "Mommy *doesn't have* ten empty spools of thread, two empty oatmeal drums, three dozen popsicle sticks, and fifteen bottle caps."

---

2   To the great relief of parents and children across America, a vaccine for chicken pox did, at long last, become available in 1995.

That's when Katy asked if she might be allowed out of the apartment to accompany me down the hall when I emptied the trash.

"Please," she begged, digging behind her ear.

"Well, okay," I reluctantly agreed. "But try not to scratch."

Not wanting to risk exposing our neighbors to the pox, we planned our twenty-yard trek to the incinerator chute like a scene out of *The Great Escape*. ("I'll watch the elevator! You guard the turn in the hall!")

Bad idea.

"Stay back!" I cried as the nice young mother in apartment 503 came wheeling around the corner with her newborn baby girl. *"Chicken pox!"*

I watched with dismay as the mother's expression shifted from open-faced friendliness, to confusion, and finally—her eyes falling upon Katy's pink-spotted face and arms—to utter horror.

"I'm *so* sorry," I apologized, grabbing Katy's hand and racing down the hall back to our apartment.

Will that new baby get the pox? Won't she get the pox? Poor little baby. Poor new mother. Poor Katy. More to the point, poor *me!*

Sometimes, God, being a mom is not much fun ...

Absently, I pull at the crust of one of the sandwiches on the bench and toss it toward the cluster of hungry pigeons now milling around my feet. As if a single organism, the birds flock toward the crust, stabbing at it with their beaks and flinging it up in the air like a volleyball. With each toss, the crust grows smaller and smaller, until suddenly it is gone. Still the pigeons continue to peck-peck-peck at the pavement. Funny how it never occurs to them to look up, where—less than two feet above their bowed and bobbing iridescent green necks—awaits the feast that is Katy's and Brinck's lunch. And suddenly, unexpectedly, I'm seized by the most curious thought.

How like those old pigeons I am! So focused am I on the worrisome, tedious, tiresome, frustrating, and inconvenient aspects of motherhood that I fail to see the larger reality that surrounds me. How can I dwell on cotton balls and calamine lotion when all around me—in the clear, sweet air, the cloudless sky, the buds bursting on the trees, the laughter of my children—the city sings of spring, and hope, and healing, and new beginnings?

Suddenly the children are at the bench, their noisy arrival sending the pigeons up and away in a flutter of sooty wings.

Soon enough, the pox will pass. Soon enough, my children will be well.

Soon enough.

Thank You, Father, for all Your many blessings! Help me to keep my eyes looking ever-upward so I can see the feast of hope, and healing, and love, and joy that You spread out for me every day.

How to Grow Your Child's Faith in God

Faith, a wise person once said, should be as natural as breathing. Indeed, all we have to do is look at the faith of a small child to be reminded how as human beings we come into this world hardwired to believe in, trust, and love our Creator. As a friend of mine likes to say, "Children are like little ambassadors from God, eager to teach us about His heavenly kingdom."

As every parent knows, children possess a very active inner life and can be surprisingly curious about religious and spiritual matters. Consider a few of the questions my daughter, Katy, and son, Brinck, asked when they were young:

- "If God is invisible, how can I know He is real?"
- "When Jesus was born, was it before or after the dinosaurs?"
- "How can God and Jesus be the same?"
- "But my friend Alex says he doesn't believe in God."
- "Mommy, what happens to me after I die?"
- "Up in heaven, does Grandpa know it's my birthday?"

I was also surprised to observe that even at a very young age, my son and daughter were already being exposed to the darker sides of human nature. Even within their seemingly sheltered worlds of home and family, school and church, they grappled daily with complex emotions of rejection, temptation, peer pressure, guilt, anger, sadness, and loss—all part and parcel of growing up and being human, but confusing and painful nonetheless. Here are just a few examples of their struggles with painful childhood emotions:

- "Emily says she isn't my friend anymore!"
- "Megan says it's okay to say, 'Shut up.' How come you and Daddy tell me it's wrong?"
- "I know I'm not supposed to talk in the library, but when I sit next to Sarah, it's so hard not to."
- "Tracy says I'm fat. Mommy, am I fat?"
- "Sometimes, Mommy, I love my teacher more than you. I hope that doesn't make you too sad." (It did!)
- "But what if when it's my turn, I feel too shy to sit on Santa's lap?"

From the start, I knew I very much wanted Katy and Brinck to have a strong faith to help them as they grew. As a new parent, I understood that typically, a child's religious education includes enrollment in Sunday school, familiarity with the Bible, and family rituals, such as routine prayers at meals and bedtime. But over the years, I learned that's not enough. It takes a personal, intimate relationship with a loving God to breathe life and meaning into these religious traditions. Kids, like grown-ups, need faith.

So what's a parent to do?

Here are the five most helpful tips I know for helping your child grow in faith:

One: Relax!

Children enter this world with a tremendous capacity for faith. For children, believing in God is instinctive. For children, faith *is* as natural as breathing. It's not a stretch to say that kids are natural-born experts when it comes to believing in God. Jesus recognized this when He said,

"Let the little children come to me, and do not hinder them, for the kingdom of God belongs to such as these. I tell you the truth, anyone who will not receive the kingdom of God like a little child will never enter it" (Luke 18:16–17). As parents, it is not only our privilege but also our responsibility to nurture our children's God-given faith.

Two: Learn with your child …

And don't be surprised when your child teaches you! I know a woman whose father died shortly after her wedding, and over the years she continued to grieve that he would never know his grandchildren.

"Don't be sad about Grandpa," her four-year-old son said firmly one day. "Don't you know he's watching us through a hole in the clouds?"

Now clearly this is not a theologically orthodox view of the Christian afterlife. But her child spoke with such assurance, with such simple faith, that she was jolted into accepting the reality of eternal life.

As you attempt to answer your child's tougher questions, you may find that your own faith is challenged. But in the end, you will gain a clearer understanding of exactly what you believe and why. And remember, when there seems to be no satisfactory answer for a question, don't be afraid to say, "I don't know." Or "Let's look in the Bible." Or "Let's ask our pastor or minister or priest about that."

Three: Remember, actions speak louder than words.

Ouch! If you're like me, this one is always a challenge. How does your relationship with God figure in your own day-to-day life?

I knew a mom who, whenever the family's pet hamster escaped, invited God to join the search party. And in New York City, I knew a dad who, whenever he encountered a down-and-out person on the street, offered a gift of food—an apple or a sandwich from a nearby deli. When asked by his ten-year-old daughter why he did this, he answered, "Because this is what Jesus expects me to do."

Four: Pray with your child.

In addition to regular prayers at meals and bedtime, try to look for opportunities to include your child in spontaneous, conversational prayer. Talking to God in this way shows how prayer can be a part of daily life. This is the intimate, natural way that Jesus prayed. In fact, Jesus was so comfortable and close to God that when He prayed, He called His father "Abba," which in His native Aramaic language means "Daddy" or "Papa."

I'll never forget the afternoon when our daughter was in sixth grade playing soccer and one of her classmates took a terrible fall, badly twisting her ankle. The girl's mother immediately ran to her side and didn't think twice about praying out loud for her child.

Even as our kids grew older, Tom and I kept praying with them. They didn't seem to mind, especially during that most grueling and stressful of modern parenting experiences: the college application process. Many times while sitting in the car in a college admissions parking lot, we would take a moment to pray, asking God to walk alongside our child throughout his or her visit.

And I'll always remember the afternoon Katy came to me with her completed application to her favorite school.

"Mom," she said, "will you say a prayer?"

Together we placed our hands on the fat envelope and asked God for His will to be done regarding the results. It was a tremendous comfort for both of us to know that whatever the outcome was, the situation was in God's capable and loving hands. Wouldn't you know, Katy not only wound up graduating from this particular school, but it is also where she met the wonderful young man who would become her husband!

Five: Tell your child what you believe.

Don't be shy about this! And pay attention to the inner nudging of God's Holy Spirit. One Christmas Eve when Katy was five years old and I was tucking her into bed, I found myself gently steering our talk from Santa Claus and the presents under the tree to what we were actually celebrating. Without planning it, I suddenly found myself telling Katy who Jesus was for me and the story—a simplified version—of how He had come into my life. Then we prayed one of the simplest, most profound prayers I know: "Jesus, I love You and believe in You. Please come into my heart now, live in me, and be my friend and savior."

It is important to remember that our children really do believe and take to heart what we tell them. Consider, for example, the ancient and beautiful phrase in the Christian sacrament of Holy Baptism that promises our children are "sealed by the Holy Spirit and marked as Christ's own forever." Isn't that beautiful? It's a phrase I continue to repeat to my kids—even now that they're grown—to remind them of their identity as people of faith.

Just the other day, our now-grown son, Brinck, was pulling out of the driveway after a weekend visit home. As I waved good-bye, I impulsively called, "Remember, Brinck, you're sealed by the Holy Spirit and marked as Christ's own forever!"

"Yeah, yeah, Mom." He rolled his eyes. "I know."

He knows, I thought. My spirit soared. For this mortal, flawed, ever-anxious, ever-praying mother, this was not only good news. It was the best news I could ever hope for.

The Gospel for Kids

Growing up isn't easy. Today, more than ever, children need to be informed and reassured that *God is real*, that *He personally loves them*, and that *He has a unique purpose for each of their lives*.

I was nineteen years old—a bewildered and unformed college sophomore in the turbulent early 1970s—before I ever heard the Christian Gospel presented in a clear, easy-to-grasp, meaningful way. The word *gospel* literally means "good news." To this day, it is that moment—the night I first heard the Gospel and asked Jesus Christ into my heart—that remains the single most important, life-transforming, personally helpful event in my life.

What a shame, I've often thought, *that so many years had to pass before I first heard the Gospel and believed.* Even as a small child—*especially as a child*—might not I have benefited from the priceless gift of a personal relationship with Jesus?

It was in direct response to questions about God and Jesus posed by my daughter and son when they were young that I wrote this Gospel for children. Because it is for children, it is written in clear, easy-to-understand language for youngsters of all ages and all denominations. And because it is for children, I emphasize the unique nature of Jesus as the ultimate friend.

It is this, after all, that every person, at every age, yearns for …
A friend.
A real friend.

A friend who is faithful. A friend who is all-forgiving. A friend you can trust. A friend whose presence makes you feel deep-down good inside. A friend who will laugh with you and cry with you. A friend to whom you can call out anytime, anywhere, and know he will be there.

This is the friend I've come to know and love in Jesus Christ. This is the friend Jesus I hope my children and grandchildren, and—through this *Gospel for Kids*—children of all ages everywhere, will come to know and love as well.

Editor's Note: Since its original publication in 1989, *The Gospel for Kids* has been translated into nine languages and sold more than one hundred thousand copies around the world.

The Gospel for Kids

by Kathryn Slattery

For Katy and Brinck and children of all ages, everywhere ...

Long, long ago, ever so many years after the dinosaurs and two thousand years before TV, a baby boy was born in the tiny town of Bethlehem in the tiny country of Israel.

We know this is true.

It is not a myth or legend or fairy tale.

It is an honest-to-goodness historical fact.

But because it happened so many years ago, long before there were things like personal computers and the Internet, we don't know for sure the exact day this baby boy was born. Or the exact address.

We do know that He was born in a stable, which is like a small barn.

He was born in a stable because hospitals hadn't been invented yet and because there was no room at any of Bethlehem's inns for the baby's family, which was visiting from out of town.

The baby's mother was named Mary. Her husband was a man named Joseph. But many months earlier, before Mary even knew she was going to have a baby, a beautiful angel named Gabriel visited her to share this great mystery:

"You are going to bear a son," Gabriel announced to the astonished Mary. "And His true Father will be God in heaven."

As Gabriel instructed, Mary named her baby boy Jesus, which means *Savior*, or "One who saves the people."

And to this day, Jesus remains *the most important person who ever lived* in the history of our world.

Why is Jesus so important?

Because of who He is and because of the extraordinary things He said and did during His time here on earth.

What are some of the things Jesus said and did?

Well, for starters, Jesus said He was God's very own Son—and everyone knows how important God is!

Jesus was so close to God that when He prayed, or talked to God, He used the word *"Abba,"* which in Jesus's native Aramaic language means "Daddy" or "Papa."

Jesus said that God, His Father in heaven, had sent Him to planet earth to bring people love and forgiveness and peace and happiness. He said His Father, God, had sent Him to show people everywhere once and for all what God was really like.

When Jesus was born, it was as though God Himself put skin on and came crashing into human history!

Until Jesus was born, you see, no one had ever really seen God.

No one was sure what God was really like.

Was God friendly? Or was He grouchy? Was God happy? Or was He gloomy? Did God cry? Did God laugh? Did God even think or care much about His people at all? Or was He too busy doing important things like keeping the stars up in the sky and the planets from bumping into each other?

Jesus said that God cares about each and every one of us—and that includes you and me—*a lot.*

Jesus said, "Listen to what I say, and watch what I do. I will show you what My Father, God, is like and how much He cares about you."

To show people what God is like, Jesus did a lot of loving, kindhearted things like make sick people well, and lame people walk, and blind people see, and deaf people hear. Once He even brought a dead person named Lazarus back to life!

When people were sad, Jesus cried with them. When people were happy, He laughed with them. He was a most excellent friend.

Jesus did all these things to show how much God loves and cares for us. Jesus did all these things so that people everywhere—and that includes you and me—would believe that He really, truly was God's Son and so that we would believe in God too.

There is another very important thing about Jesus, and that is that *He loved children.*

Though Jesus never got married and had children of His own, He deeply loved all the boys and girls He met. And the children loved Him back.

Grown-ups, Jesus said, could learn a lot from children.

Children, He explained, were natural-born experts when it came to believing in God.

"Let all the children come to Me and believe in Me and in My Father, God," Jesus said. "And as for you grown-ups: You try and be a little more like children this way yourselves, understand?"

Many of the grown-ups understood what Jesus was trying to teach them and loved Him.

But others didn't.

And when Jesus was still a young man, just thirty-three years old, He was killed—put to death on a wooden cross—by fearful, unhappy people who didn't understand the things He said and did. Jesus was killed by people who just couldn't find it in their hearts to believe Him. Jesus was killed by people who had forgotten how to be like children in their hearts.

Now since Jesus was God's Son, He could have stopped these people from killing Him. But He didn't. By choosing to give up His life, He took upon Himself the punishment for all the bad things people do and think.

Jesus died to save everyone on earth who would believe in Him. That's why He is called our Savior.

How sad people were on the day Jesus died!

His mother and brothers and sisters and friends—all of them missed Him terribly. They cried and cried.

If only Jesus could somehow come back and be with us, they thought.

But that was impossible. Never again would they hear the sound of Jesus's laughter, listen to His stories, or feel His big, strong hugs.

They took His broken, lifeless body and laid it gently in a tomb, which was like a small, dark room with a dirt floor carved into the side of a grassy hill. The strongest men rolled a big rock over the opening to the tomb, and then—their hearts nearly breaking with sorrow—they all walked away.

Early in the morning three days after Jesus died, Jesus's friend—a woman named Mary Magdalene—set off to visit the tomb where Jesus's body had been laid. But when she arrived, the big stone that had covered the opening to the tomb had been rolled away. Stranger still, the tomb was empty. Where had the body of her beloved Jesus gone?

It was soon after that Mary made the most wonderful, important, extraordinary discovery …

*Jesus was **alive**!*

The tomb was empty because Jesus—in the most mysterious, awesome, miraculous way—was no longer dead, *but had come back to **life**!*

How happy everyone was to see and be with Jesus again!

Once again He talked and laughed with His mother, family, and friends. He even had a picnic on the beach with some of his best friends. Once again they all gathered around Him and listened to His stories.

Jesus said that soon He would be going back to heaven to live with His Father, God. But before He left, He had some very good news.

Everyone leaned forward and listened carefully.

"The good news," said Jesus, "is that because I have come back to life, you, too, can live forever with Me and My Father, God, in heaven. God loves you so much, He wants this for you. He wants you to believe in Him and Me. He wants to forgive you when you make mistakes. He wants you to live with Him forever."

Jesus explained to His family and friends that because they loved and believed Him, after their lives on earth ended, they would find themselves alive in heaven with God and Him.

It will be such a happy time … like a big birthday party!

This is because everyone in heaven is happy and healthy. Everyone in heaven has new bodies that live forever, and there is no more sadness or crying or pain.

"In heaven," said Jesus, "God will wipe away every tear from every eye."

There is one last thing Jesus told His family and friends before He returned to heaven to live with God.

Jesus told them that although He could no longer stay with them in person, God had arranged a special way that He could stay with them in their hearts.

"I will send you My Holy Spirit," said Jesus. "He will live in your hearts and teach you, and guide you, and comfort you—just the way I've been able to do while I've been with you here on earth."

True to His promise, that is exactly what Jesus did.

Even today, right now, Jesus can be alive in our hearts through His Holy Spirit.

Even today, it is possible to listen to His voice … hear His laughter … even feel His hugs.

Do you know what Jesus wants for you right now, more than anything?

Right now, Jesus wants to live in your heart.

More than anything, Jesus wants to be your friend.

He wants to be the kind of friend who will help you know right from wrong. The kind of friend who will forgive you when you make mistakes and love you no matter what. The kind of friend who is fun to be with and will make you feel deep-down good inside.

Jesus wants to be the kind of friend you can talk to when you're sad, when you're happy, when you're lonely, when you're scared—anytime at all!

Yes, more than anything, Jesus wants to be your Savior and friend—the best you ever had.

If you're not sure Jesus is living in your heart, would you like to ask Him in to be your friend?

It's easy.

All you have to do is call His name and let Him know. Like this:

"Hi, Jesus! I just want to let You know that I believe in You and in Your Father, God. Thank You for forgiving me when I make mistakes and for loving me the way You do. Please come into my heart now and live in me and be my friend. I love You, Jesus. And I'm really excited about being Your friend too."

Once you've prayed this prayer (for that's all prayer really is—talking to Jesus!), you will be beginning a new adventure in your life unlike any other. Wherever you go, whatever you do, Jesus will be with you, living in your heart, helping and loving you.

Whenever you want Him, just call His name. Say, "Hi, Jesus!" and He will be with you—listening, caring, and being the *best friend* you ever had.

Now that you've reached the end of this story, you are about to begin a brand-new story.

A real, true-life story that begins here and now …

In your heart.

It is the story of your new life and the special friendship that's yours forever with Jesus.

Have fun!

How to Give Good Gifts to Your Kids at Christmastime

In the Bible we read how God *loves* to give good gifts to His children (Matthew 7:10–11). And isn't that just how we feel toward our children too? Where does this generous gift-giving impulse come from? It comes from God, *our* Creator Father! Because we are made in His image, He has planted His generous, gift-giving nature in our hearts to encourage and bless our children.

Despite the increasing secularization and commercialization of Christmas, there are an infinite variety of ways to breathe spiritual life into this important Christian holiday. It helps that the birth of Jesus is a relatively simple idea for children to grasp. Nativity scenes, carols, and pageants all help to reinforce the idea that "Jesus is the reason for the season" and make it easier to keep Santa Claus in perspective.

Setting up a crèche, for example, offers one of the best ways I've found to have fun while simultaneously nurturing your child's faith.

In our family, we wait until midnight to put the baby Jesus in His manger. I will always remember the Christmas morning when our two children were as excited about the appearance of the baby Jesus in His crib as they were about Santa's gifts under the tree … well, *almost*. But it was a start!

When my friend Mary sets up her family's nativity scene, she places the three wise men and their camels at the far corner of the house and then moves them closer and closer to the nativity scene with each

Merry Christmas from the Slatterys!

passing day. On Christmas morning, the wise men are still half a room away. "Still on their long journey," she explains to her children, "still following the star in the East." The arrival of the wise men twelve days later on Epiphany, with their gifts of gold, frankincense, and myrrh for the Christ Child, is celebrated with great excitement and a special Epiphany tea party with star-shaped cookies.

I have another friend whose family has the tradition of ending their Christmas dinner with a special homemade birthday cake for Jesus, decorated with a sprig of holly and a single white candle. They even sing the "Happy Birthday" song to Jesus before allowing the youngest person at the table to blow out the candle.

Do you put out stockings for Santa to fill? If so, this provides endless possibilities for creative, faith-based gift giving. When our two children were young, I found a set of Bible storybooks for our son and came across a tiny mustard-seed necklace for our daughter. Then I tucked these faith-filled presents between the candy canes and other holiday treats in their stockings. Over the years, I've added inspirational CDs and videos, Scripture stickers, prayer journals, bookmarks, and books.

Lots and lots of books! Books are *the best!* There are *so many* wonderful books with helpful, wholesome, spiritual messages for children.

For example, *The Runaway Bunny* by Margaret Wise Brown is actually a very faith-based story, with its reassuring message of a mother who would search endlessly to find her child, as are the children's classics *The Velveteen Rabbit* by Margery Williams and C. S. Lewis's *The Chronicles of Narnia*. For older children, there are Madeleine L'Engle's *A Wrinkle in Time* and J. R. R. Tolkien's *The Hobbit* and *Lord of the Rings* trilogy. In fact, I am so enthusiastic about giving books that help to encourage and nurture young people's faith that I eventually wound up writing my own book for children, *If I Could Ask God Anything: Awesome Bible Answers for Curious Kids*.

So as Christmastime approaches, get creative! Be inspired! Talk to your friends about their family traditions and gift-giving ideas, too. Most of all, access your own unique, inner gift-giving nature, which has been generously planted in your heart by God, who loves you and your children more than you can ever imagine.

And may your Christmas be extravagantly, abundantly, lovingly, and surprisingly blessed in every way!

Brinck as an angel!

All I Want for Christmas . . .

It was 6:30 p.m. on Friday, December 23—the eve of Christmas weekend. Cookies were baking in the oven, apple cider was bubbling on the stove, four-year-old Brinck and seven-year-old Katy were breathlessly comparing their lists for Santa, and I was getting a little frantic. Okay, a *lot* frantic. From now on it was going to be nonstop cooking, last-minute shopping, and entertaining. The Christmas tree was shedding like a cat, half our Christmas cards remained unsent, and I hadn't wrapped a single gift.

I reached for a package of festive paper plates and yanked the plastic wrapping open with my teeth. *Ouch!* There was a sharp pain at the front of my mouth and a strange sensation of something giving way. An object clattered on the tile floor. An earring perhaps? But even before my fingers could fly up to touch my ears, I grasped the awful truth.

"My tooth!" I wailed. "My tooth fell out!"

My tongue probed the empty space where my front tooth should have been. I got down on my hands and knees and peered underneath the dishwasher. There it was, grinning back at me, it seemed. I reached into the dusty darkness to retrieve the tooth—a crown, actually—and as I turned it slowly in my hand, my heart sank. There, embedded in dental cement, was the broken-off stub of my real tooth, which for the past twelve years had held the crown in place.

I ran to the dining room mirror. All that remained of my tooth was a jagged nib at the gum line.

Oh, no! This can't be happening!

Tomorrow was Christmas Eve. At four o'clock in the afternoon was the much-anticipated children's service and nativity pageant at our church, where Brinck was going to be an angel and Katy was thrilled to be playing the role of Mary. Tom and I had invited my sister, Laurrie, and my mother, plus out-of-town guests, for Christmas Eve supper. How could I face everyone with a missing front tooth?

I called my dentist, Madeline Apfel, at her office.

Oh, God, I prayed. *Please let her be there.*

But all I got was her answering machine.

I called our children's dentist. I called my sister's dentist. I called dentists listed in the yellow pages. I even called a dentist in New Jersey. At the start of each message, my voice was controlled and brave. But before the end of each message, I dissolved into incoherent blubbering. Not helping matters was the fact that a newly acquired lisp made my name almost impossible to pronounce.

"*Thlattery!*" I heard myself saying. "Thpelled with an *eth*—ath in 'Thylvethter Cat.'"

As a last resort, I called New York City's Emergency Dental Service Hot Line. But on a Friday night of a holiday weekend, no one was available to help.

"I'm sorry," a weary voice said. "You'll have to call back Monday morning."

My only hope, I was told, might be found at one of two hospitals in the city that had an emergency room dentist on call. Tom stayed at home with the kids, and Laurrie agreed to go with me to Beth Israel Hospital. When we got there, the resident dentist confirmed my worst fears: although he had state-of-the-art emergency room equipment that could wire my jaws shut if I'd been in a wreck, he couldn't help with "routine" work that had to be done by my own dentist.

"It could be worse," he said, trying to cheer me up. "The only thing that's hurt is your vanity."

"It's *not* just my vanity," I wailed to Laurrie as we trudged home in the winter dark. "A part of me is missing. It's as though I've suddenly gone bald or found myself naked in a crowd. I don't want to be laughed at, and I don't want to be lectured. I want *thympathy!*"

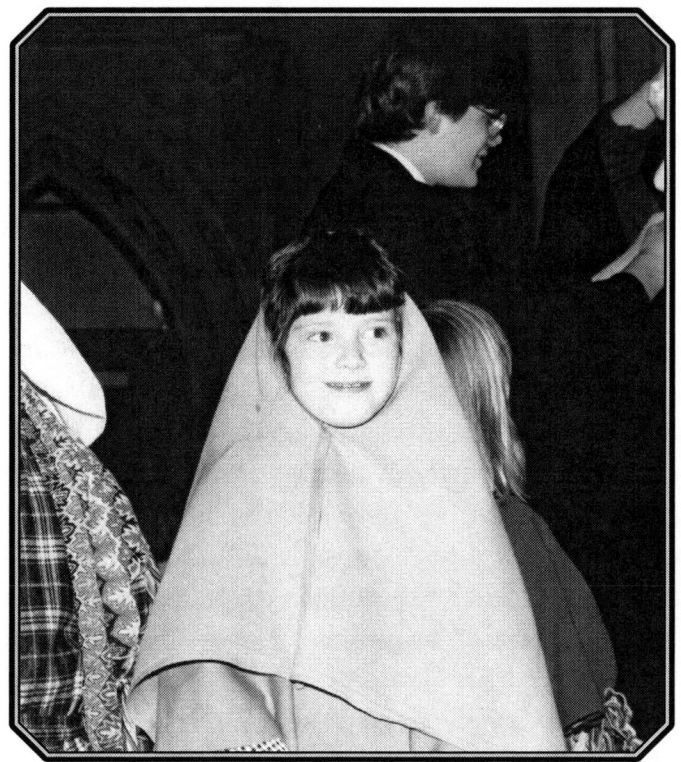

Katy dressed up as Mary for the Christmas Pageant

But sympathy was hard to come by—even from Tom.

"Aw, c'mon, Kitty," he said as I slumped through the front door with the bad news. "It's just a tooth."

Easy for him to say. A man who never had a cavity in his life.

That night I slept fitfully and awoke exhausted on Christmas Eve day. As the morning dragged on, I grew more gloomy and self-absorbed. The empty socket where my tooth should have been was like a black hole, sucking every happy holiday thought from my mind. The Christmas pageant was just hours away. What a sorry soul I was to allow a silly missing tooth to put a damper on what was supposed to be one of the most joyful nights of the year.

It was noon when the telephone rang.

"This is Maddy," a familiar voice said. "I just checked my answering machine and got your message from last night. Do you still need help?"

Maddy! Maddy Apfel, my dentist!

"I can see you at two-thirty," she said. "I can't promise anything, but we'll see what we can do."

Maddy's office was a five-minute walk away on Washington Square. As I walked along lower Fifth Avenue, I thought about the woman turning on the lights in her office and waiting for me. Maddy was unmarried, a striking woman with wide-set eyes and a luxurious mane of blonde-highlighted hair. Sometimes I thought she had to be the most glamorous dentist in New York. For sure, she was the only dentist who cared enough to drop everything to help a patient in need on Christmas Eve. I apologized profusely for inconveniencing her.

"You know, Kitty," she said, clipping a paper bib around my neck, "maybe like yourself, I've got tons to do. I've got company coming for dinner, my apartment's a mess, my tablecloth needs ironing, I haven't wrapped a single gift, and I was beginning to panic. But you know what? It doesn't matter. Your call helped me put everything in perspective."

She smiled. "In a funny way, just knowing you need my help is the best Christmas present anyone could give me."

As I leaned back in the leather chair and opened my mouth, I mulled over Maddy's words.

My need—a gift? But then, why not? If Maddy obtained joy and satisfaction from helping me, my need was indeed a gift. I began to relax for the first time in days. In fact, I was almost glad my tooth fell out. In a way, this whole episode had served to help two frantic women put things in perspective.

For the next ninety minutes, Maddy hummed along merrily to Christmas carols on the radio as she installed a temporary crown. She told me that I would have to return again for more work, but at least I would have a front tooth to get me through the holidays.

At precisely four o'clock, I slipped into the church pew between Tom and Mom.

"Everything okay?" whispered Tom.

My smile was all the answer he needed.

Emmett McCallister's Christmas Eve: An Old Tale Retold

Santa Claus! Toys! Candy! With the ever-increasing commercialization of Christmas, what's a parent to do when it comes to explaining the real meaning of this most holy Christian holiday? The heartwarming story of Emmett McCallister, a crusty old New Englander whose heart is miraculously touched and transformed one snowy Christmas Eve, is written for families to gather around and enjoy together as a gentle reminder of the true "reason for the season" and of God's great love for all His children throughout the year.

Emmett McCallister's Christmas Eve
An Old Tale Retold

by Kathryn Slattery

Emmett McCallister sighed restlessly as he poked at the smoldering remains of what had been a raging blaze in his fireplace. He debated whether to toss on another log or turn out the lights and go to bed. It was Christmas Eve, and his wife Martha had gone to midnight Mass.

"Emmett, dear," Martha had whispered softly while wrapping a woolen muffler tightly around her neck, "won't you consider coming with me tonight? It's going to be a beautiful Christmas service—complete with carols and candles. I think you really might enjoy it."

"No, Martha," Emmett had replied, shaking his head stubbornly. "No church. No carols. No candles. You know how I feel about Christmas. I think it's a lot of hogwash." For a moment, noticing the pained look in Martha's eyes, Emmett felt badly. But then he stiffened, determined not to let his emotions get the better of him.

"Now you be careful," he said gruffly, offering his wife a perfunctory peck on the cheek. "It looks as though we might be in for some nasty weather."

Indeed, a bitter wind now whistled through the cracks of the McCallisters' old New England farmhouse. Emmett peered through the century-old panes of glass as the howling wind whipped the white, falling snow into a frenzy.

Wouldn't you know, he thought, reaching for a log and thrusting it into the fireplace. *A nor'easter, no less. And just in time for Christmas.*

"Christmas," he muttered scornfully under his breath, as though irritated by the word itself. "Hogwash."

With a "Harrumph!" worthy of Ebenezer Scrooge, Emmett reached up to straighten his prized collection of hand-carved and painted decoys that lined the rough-hewn wooden mantle above the fireplace.

The firelight flickering in the glass amber eyes of one mallard drake seemed to make the bird come alive. Gently, Emmett stroked the duck's iridescent green head, letting his fingers trace the distinctive white ring that circled its neck like a cleric's collar.

While Emmett may have hated Christmas, he loved birds.

―――

Emmett's interest in birds began when, as a boy of seven, he had nursed an injured baby robin back to health by hand-feeding it wriggly worms and grubs with tweezers and keeping it warm in one of his father's fleece-lined woolen slippers. Ever since, Emmett had remained fascinated by birds—by their paradoxically delicate yet high-performance anatomy ... by their wondrous ability to fly ... by their melodious songs ... and by their mysterious instinct that enabled them to journey thousands of miles in uncanny synchronization with nature's changing rhythms. Now Emmett's large yard was studded with assorted handmade birdhouses, birdbaths, feeders, and suet bags.

"Honest to Pete," Martha was prone to comment upon Emmett's return from one of his frequent trips to the local feed store—his arms aching under the weight of twenty-five-pound sacks of cracked corn and sunflower seeds—"sometimes I think you like those birds more than people."

"Sometimes I do," he would reply.

―――

Leaving his collection of decoys, Emmett returned to his easy chair. Piled high on the coffee table was the day's mail, for the most part a jumble of gaily colored Christmas cards.

For unto you is born this day a Savior, read one.

And the Word became flesh, and dwelt among us, read another.

"Hogwash," muttered Emmett, pushing the cards aside to reach for his favorite bird magazine. But as he pulled the magazine onto his lap and saw its cover, his face fell.

It couldn't be said that the cover illustration was offensive in any way—it was a fairly typical rendering of two cardinals perched on a snow-covered pine bough. But the picture's theme was obvious: *Christmas.* Emmett's blood pressure began to rise. He felt betrayed. And angry. Even his favorite magazine had sold out to the holiday season. Letting the magazine drop to the floor, he leaned back in his chair and closed his eyes.

What is it about Christmas that bothers me so? he wondered. *What is it about this time of year that makes others so happy?*

Christmas, for Emmett, had been tolerable when his children were small and living at home. He had no problem accepting Santa, and Rudolph, and stockings hung over the fireplace, and all the other trappings of the season. But when it came to the heart of the holiday—when it came to the story of a baby called Jesus born two thousand years ago—that's when Emmett became impatient.

What can such talk about God becoming human be besides foolish religious prattle? he thought. *And even if the story is true, why should such an event be necessary? Besides,* he fumed, *what has this Jesus ever done for me?*

The only time Emmett felt the least bit sorrowful for his inability to enjoy Christmas was when he was reminded—on nights like tonight—of how important this Jesus seemed to be to his wife, Martha. Emmett loved Martha dearly, and it bothered him when he perceived, however dimly, the great spiritual gulf that yawned between them. Sometimes he sensed that something was missing in their relationship because he didn't share his wife's interest in knowing Jesus. But being a man of few words, such feelings had always been too vague and fuzzy for him to articulate.

Suddenly there was a commotion at the parlor window. A frantic fluttering of wings, piercing cries of distress—Emmett knew the sounds all too well. In a flash, he was up, his face pressed against the cold glass, his eyes searching the dark night. Illuminated by the glare of the garage floodlight, he saw what he was looking for—a small band of starlings lost in the storm. Three of the dozen or so birds had flown into the parlor window. Stunned by the impact, they now flopped about helplessly on the ground, their panicked movements digging them ever deeper into the fast-drifting snow.

Reaching for his windbreaker and pulling on his boots, Emmett stepped out onto the front porch. The starlings grew even more distressed.

"No, no," murmured Emmett. "Please don't be scared. Don't be frightened. I'm here to help you. Please let me help you."

The starlings needed shelter. And fast. For the birds to remain unprotected in the bitter weather for much longer would surely result in their death.

Shielding his face against the blowing snow with his arm, Emmett pushed himself into the gale-force wind and trudged the thirty-foot distance to his garage. He opened the door. If only he could guide the starlings into the garage, he reasoned, then they would be safe.

But how to do it? he wondered as he made his way back to the troubled birds. *The starlings are so frightened already; why should they trust me?*

For the next ten minutes, like an ungainly sheepdog, Emmett did his best to round up the starlings and herd them toward the garage. But his efforts were futile. There were too many birds. Like a shepherd needs a staff, Emmett needed some kind of tool that would help him in his task.

He returned to the house to get a broom.

But to Emmett's dismay, this approach met with results even more disastrous than the first. The starlings, already frightened and confused, responded in sheer terror to the broom, scattering in all directions. Many fell into deep snowbanks.

Heartsick and exhausted, Emmett finally realized the situation was hopeless. By morning, the starlings would all be dead.

Returning to the house, he hung his jacket, wet with snow, on the row of wooden pegs by the front door and kicked off his boots. He returned to his easy chair, and there, hanging his head in his hands, he wept. Bitterly he wept. As he hadn't wept since he was a boy, Emmett cried for his lost starlings.

Some time later, when he could cry no longer, Emmett heaved a long, shuddery sigh and closed his eyes.

"Dear God," he murmured, "if only I could become a starling so I could show those helpless creatures the way to safety and shelter and life. If only I could become one of them, then they would trust me. They would listen to me. Then—and only then—we could communicate with each other in a way never before possible."

Slowly, Emmett opened his eyes.

Irresistibly, his gaze was drawn to the pile of Christmas cards on the coffee table in front of him. For the second time that evening, he considered their messages:

For unto you is born this day a Savior ...

And the Word became flesh, and dwelt among us ...

And then a strange thing happened to Emmett.

No longer did the sight of Christmas cards annoy him. No longer did he despise this holiday season. For now, at long last, Emmett understood.

Just as Emmett loved and cared for his starlings so much that he wanted to become one of them to save them, so God loved humankind so much that He sent His only Son, Jesus, into the world to reveal Himself and save all who would believe.

How simple, Emmett thought. *How wonderful!*

"Thank You, God," he whispered, trembling with excitement at his new discovery. "Thank You for loving me so much that You sent Jesus to be born to guide and protect and save me. Thank You for helping me understand the true meaning of Christmas."

Abruptly, Emmett jumped at the sound of his name. It was his wife Martha, home from midnight Mass.

"Emmett!" she cried, her voice high-pitched with excitement. "*Emmett!*"

"What is it?" Emmett answered.

Martha appeared in the parlor, her face flushed from running. Her boots left wet tracks on the hardwood floor, and she hadn't bothered to remove her coat or muffler.

"Emmett McCallister!" she exclaimed. "What are all those birds doing in our garage?"

"Birds?" asked Emmett with a puzzled look.

"You heard me," said Martha. "Birds. More than a dozen. Starlings, I think. They're all perched up in the rafters, singing up a storm. And I'm afraid some of them must have gotten into your feed bags—there's seed spilled all over the floor. Honestly, Emmett," she shook her head, "I don't mind your birds as long as they stay outside. But when you start bringing them inside …"

"Starlings, you say?" Emmett's face was incredulous. "More than a dozen?" It was too good to be true. Nothing short of God's own hand could have guided those half-frozen and confused birds into the garage.

"Yes," replied Martha. "That's what I said." She paused. "Emmett, you look strange. Emmett—are you all right?"

"All right?" cried Emmett, grabbing Martha around her plump waist and spinning her in a dizzying circle. "All right? Martha, my dear, I've never been better. You may find this hard to believe, but there's been a miracle tonight. An honest-to-goodness miracle right here in our own house!"

"Miracle?" asked Martha skeptically. "But Emmett, you don't believe in miracles. You don't even believe in Christmas. What in heaven's name are you talking about?"

"There's been a miracle," repeated Emmett emphatically. "A Christmas miracle."

Chuckling, Emmett took Martha by the hand and led her out the front door, toward the garage.

"Come on," he said. "Let's go have a look at those starlings, and I'll tell you all about it."

My Christmas Angel

Photo credit: Deborah Ory

Today, as I go into the closet to take down the boxes of Christmas ornaments, I find myself thinking of that gloomy day last January when I put them up there on the shelf. I see myself standing in the living room, looking about me, feeling wistful

Gone is the gumdrop-roofed gingerbread house on the sideboard and the miniature blue porcelain crèche with its mysteriously iridescent baby Jesus. Gone are the boughs of evergreen, the holly sprigs, the bunches of red berries that poked from behind every mirror and frame.

Gone are the candles, the aroma of cider and pine. Gone, and missed most sorely, is that exquisite sense of anticipation, that feeling that something wonderful is about to happen.

All that remains of Christmas are a few dried needles somehow missed by the vacuum. One last cardboard box, on which I've scribbled "XMAS," waits to be closed and put away with the others crowding the closet's top shelf. And the angel. My Christmas angel.

He's a cherub. Bronze, with stubby wings. I purchased him quite by chance at a secondhand store one rainy winter afternoon. Now, I look at him standing on tippy-toes, his chubby arms—so like those of our own baby boy—stretching heavenward. What is it that he sees? The wonder and mystery of our Lord's birth, I like to think.

He's quite heavy, not fragile at all. Still, as though he were made of the finest bone china, I wrap him in yards and yards of tissue and gently push him deep into the box. There he will lie until next year, snug among the children's Christmas stockings with their glue and glitter names, oblivious to the cycle of birthdays, holidays, and other small pleasures the coming months will bring.

Before closing the box, I take one last, lingering look around our house, and a familiar sadness washes over me. A home after Christmas, stripped of its decorations, seems barren, empty. Despite the ubiquitous clutter of papers, knickknacks, and stray toys, I sense that something is lacking. My heart, it occurs to me, might be likened to our home: my heart, without Christ's indwelling spirit, is barren and empty. But with Christ's spirit, it is abundant and expectant.

Suddenly, impulsively, I reach into the box and retrieve my little friend. Racing toward the living room, I set my angel on the table behind the sofa.

And there, shaded by a pastel spray of silken wildflowers, he has remained, on tippy-toes, with arms and gaze upraised …

A winsome reminder of the spirit of Christmas in our home this whole year long.

How to Be a Great Godparent

It all happened so fast. My best friend Sandy had just telephoned from Florida to ask if I would consider being godmother to her second child, a newborn son.

Godmother! I was honored. I was flattered. I'd never been asked to be a godmother before.

"Sure," I replied easily.

"You don't have to answer right away," Sandy said. "Being a godparent is a serious responsibility. Maybe you'd like to think it over for a few days, maybe even pray about it."

"Don't be silly," I laughed. "I'd love to be Josh's godmother."

With some unease, I sensed that through one simple phone call my identity had taken on a new, uncertain dimension. As mother of two, I was familiar with plain old garden-variety motherhood. But *godmother*—this was different. This was …

And then it hit me. I hadn't the foggiest idea what being a godparent meant. What was it Sandy had said about godparenting being a "serious responsibility"? The way she talked, her request had more to do with Josh than with honoring me. Clearly her expectations were high. But what exactly did she expect?

I thought of my own godmother, my mother's best friend from her college days. Growing up, our families lived a thousand miles apart. On the few occasions when our paths crossed, I remembered her as a warm and friendly woman. When I was very young, she sent me Christmas presents—sometimes a doll, sometimes a book. Still, I couldn't recall that she had ever done anything that set her apart as a godmother.

Well, there was no turning back now. For better or worse, I'd impulsively said yes to Sandy's request.

Father, I said a simple prayer, *please teach me what it means to be a godparent.*

Over the next several weeks, I set out to discover everything I could about godparenting. I had been raised as a Protestant, and my friend Sandy was Roman Catholic, so I talked to a number of pastors and priests. Books on the subject are surprisingly hard to find. I also talked to friends—godparents and godchildren alike—to learn from their experiences. And what I discovered was fascinating.

The tradition of godparenting among Christians is an ancient one going back to the days of the early church, when believers were persecuted and when life expectancies in general were much shorter than they are today.

While modern-day believers in America are not persecuted as the early church once was, it could be said that the healthy growth and development of our children's faith is threatened as never before by the cumulative effect of society's ills: widespread divorce; broken homes; rampant materialism; both parents working out of economic necessity rather than choice; lack of parental supervision; parental mental illness; alcohol and drug abuse; parental physical, sexual, and emotional abuse; and the desensitization of our children to violence and sex via unsupervised viewing of inappropriate television, videos, movies, and the Internet.

In other words, kids today need all the help they can get! Over and over I was astonished to hear from clergy and laypeople alike that something so old-fashioned as good godparents practicing good godparenting could make a powerful difference.

In the New Testament, in the book of Acts, I read about whole households being baptized into faith, including infants, children, and servants. Traditionally, the godparent acts as a steward of faith for the newly baptized child, serving as an added assurance (in addition to the parents' efforts) that the child will be raised to understand fully his or her relationship to God through a personal, saving faith in Jesus Christ and involvement in the church.

Today many godparents work to achieve this same blessed goal. Unfortunately, others still wrongly perceive the role as a purely social convention, a way for new parents to honor a family member or friend. With that viewpoint, they lose the extra spiritual dimension to the relationship that grants a godparent license to reach out and be something more to the child than an aunt or uncle or "Mom's best friend." In fact, I learned of several cases in which it was the godparent who made the difference in a child's coming to faith.

As a godmother, I learned that it would be my right (and responsibility!) over the years to pray for Josh, to introduce him to Christian concepts, and to encourage any questions he might have about our faith. When a person becomes a godparent at a child's baptism, many churches provide a certificate that includes helpful suggestions and prayers. Much of this is very basic: pray for your godchild daily; remember your godchild with a gift on his birthday and—even more important—on the anniversary of his baptism; see that your godchild attends Sunday school and owns an age-appropriate Bible; and so on.

But it was the stories that people shared about their personal experiences as godchildren and godparents that really got to the heart of the task at hand.

One couple, over the course of two decades, had become something of experts when it came to gift-giving to their two godchildren, a boy and a girl. Seeking to emphasize the unique spiritual dimension of their relationship to the children, they made a special effort to select gifts that had a specifically religious or inspirational content. Bible storybooks and Noah's ark toys gave way to tiny gold-cross jewelry and the classic children's books by C. S. Lewis. When the children entered their teens, they received diary-like prayer journals, faith-based rock and pop music CDs, videos, and computer games.

Another friend, who was musical, had a grand time singing hymns and playing the piano with his godson.

Another woman stressed the importance of not only praying for but with her goddaughter. The first time she did this, she admitted she felt a little bit embarrassed and shy. But she persisted, convinced that the simple act of praying—or as she put it, "talking to God"—had a profound effect. It demonstrated that praying is something that she, a grown-up, did, and something that the child could do too. Later she was deeply moved when one afternoon the goddaughter, now grown and in the midst of grave marital problems, called her on the phone. "Oh, Nana," the troubled girl said, "will you pray with me? I need someone to pray with, and I knew you would understand."

But by far the most unforgettable godparent I heard of was a member of my pastor's first parish in South Carolina, nearly forty years ago. A maiden lady "of a certain age," Miss B. had no fewer than twenty-six godchildren!

Fresh out of seminary, my pastor thought that in order to do the job right, one should generally not take on the responsibility of being godparent to so many, so he was understandably skeptical when he first learned of Miss B.'s "children." But after he grew to know her well enough, one afternoon she escorted him to her room to show him the chart she kept at the foot of her bed. Big as a billboard, the chart took up the larger part of the wall; along the top were printed neatly the names of all twenty-six godchildren, and listed below in columns were their birthdays, baptism anniversaries, favorite books of the Bible, hymns, hobbies, foods, colors, latest accomplishments, and more. Miss B. updated the information daily. Her chart, she said, was the first thing she saw in the morning and the last thing she looked at when she went to bed.

This extraordinary woman kept track of every single one of her godchildren's comings and goings until her death. And in the end, she made a difference.

One young woman, now a nurse with children of her own, recalled how she treasured her relationship as Miss B.'s goddaughter. She appreciated the special notes of encouragement and gifts she had received each year on the anniversary of her baptism. And most of all, what a comfort it had been just to know she was being prayed for by her godmother every day.

Faith ... prayer ... comfort ... make a difference ... I kept hearing those words again and again. Being a godparent really was a serious responsibility, as Sandy had said. But yes, now I definitely wanted to do it.

Thank You, Father, I prayed. *Help me do a good job for Josh.*

A few days later I was sitting on the kitchen floor wrapping the small porcelain cradle medallion I had selected for Josh's baptism gift when my two children bounded into the room.

"What's that?" asked four-year-old Brinck.

"A cradle medallion for baby Josh," I said. "See, it's a picture of an angel escorting a little boy and girl over a rickety bridge in the midst of a raging storm. It shows how God's angels are protecting us all the time, even when we can't see them."

"I like it," said seven-year-old Katy. "The little boy and girl remind me of Brinck and me. How come you're sending it to Josh?"

"He's getting baptized next Sunday. Sandy asked me to be Josh's godmother, so I'm sending this to him for his first baptism present."

"Baptism?" asked Katy. "What's that?"

"Well, it's sort of like a birthday," I explained. "When you're baptized, you're born into the family of all the believers of Jesus."

"Birthday?" echoed Brinck. "Do I have a baptism birthday? Can I get a present too?"

And then a wonderful thought occurred to me.

What was to stop me from being a godmother in spirit to my own children too? For locked within the ancient tradition of godparenting was a fantastic treasure of practices and ideas for believers and the children they love and care about everywhere—a treasure that can make a difference.

"Why, yes, you two do have baptism birthdays," I said, tying the bow on Josh's gift. "Katy, as I recall, yours is in October. And Brinck, yours is in April. I'll have to look up the exact dates."

"Happy baptism birthday to us!" cried Brinck.

After all, kids these days need all the help they can get.

How to Make Easter Real for Your Kids

Jelly beans ... cellophane-wrapped baskets ... giant chocolate bunnies ...

As I spotted all the trappings of Easter in the supermarket, I thought to myself, *No wonder kids get confused about Easter!*

Explaining Christmas was a cinch. The birth of Jesus is relatively simple to grasp. Nativity scenes, carols, and pageants all reinforce the message, making it easier to keep Santa Claus in perspective. *But how to explain to my two children something as profound and mysterious as the Resurrection?*

I knew that other parents were struggling with this challenge too. In fact, I took the greatest comfort in the advice of one friend who said, "Start with the traditions you already have."

On Good Friday in our home, we always dye Easter eggs, at least three dozen. What could be a more obvious symbol of new life than eggs? Last year I told the children about a baby chick I once saw hatching in an incubator. I described how he poked his way out with his little beak. "A new life. That's what we celebrate at Easter," I explained, "the new life we have in Christ."

The next bit of inspiration came while I was shopping at our local card and gift shop. I found a set of Bible storybooks for our son, Brinck, and came across a tiny gold cross necklace for Katy. I tucked these presents between the jelly beans and chocolate-marshmallow eggs in the children's Easter baskets, and since then I've added prayer journals, inspirational CDs and videos, Scripture stickers, and bookmarks. I like the tradition of Easter baskets, especially when I can include gifts that will nurture the children's faith.

The third idea came from a contributor to *Guideposts* magazine, Posy Baker Lough. "Try something," she suggested, "to give children a good visual image of the Resurrection." She described a project at her church where the children were given caterpillars, and in the weeks leading up to Easter, the kids watched them spin cocoons and then metamorphose into butterflies. "The butterflies were released just before the Easter Sunday service," Posy said. "Afterward, when we explained to the kids that the cocoon was like Christ's death and entombment and that His Resurrection was like the beautiful butterfly, they understood."

At Easter time, images of new life are usually easy to find: crocuses and daffodils blooming, lambs gamboling in fields, birds busy making their nests, all shades of green returning to the landscape. But sometimes spring comes late (or Easter arrives early) and the holiday meets a gray, cold day. Then I think of the wonderful story my friend Alison told me.

Easter fun with Mom, Katy and Brinck!

On an unseasonably cold Easter morning when Alison was ten years old, her mother urged her to go outside to see what was in the yard. There in the snow her mother had fashioned a rainbow of hundreds of brightly-colored lollipops, sparkling in the pale sunlight like bits of stained glass. "It seemed like a miracle," Alison said, "magical, beautiful, full of mystery and wonder."

And that, I realize, is what I want more than anything else to give my children: the miracle of Easter. That first Easter Sunday was certainly God's most astonishing miracle, the resurrection of His Son, Jesus, and the promise it holds for us all—eternal life.

So finally, go to church on Easter. Put on your best clothes, take flowers from your garden, and sing all the hymns with loud and glad alleluias. *Celebrate!* Last Easter Sunday, I was delighted when the little boy sitting in front of us turned to his mother and said, "Christmas is Jesus's birthday—but Easter is everybody's birthday!"

Yes, it is. Easter is the time for you and your children—for all of us—to joyfully celebrate our new birth.

Grandma, I'll Miss You: A Child's Story about Death and New Life

Grandma, I'll Miss You is a story written to comfort children suffering the pain and loss of losing a loved one. Sharing this story with little ones during happier times will help to prepare them for life's losses. It will introduce them to the mystery of death and encourage them to view this natural and inevitable part of being human not with fear, but with a sense of hope and wonder.

The good news is that in the end, *Grandma, I'll Miss You* is not a story about death at all—but about life. Beautiful, eternal life—lived to the fullest, both here and now on earth, and forever in heaven.

Grandma, I'll Miss You
A Child's Story about Death and New Life

by Kathryn Slattery

For Katy and Brinck and children of all ages, everywhere...

Lo! I tell you a mystery. We shall not all sleep,
But we shall all be changed, in a moment,
In the twinkling of an eye...
—1 Corinthians 15:51–52

Happy and sad.

That's how Katy felt.

Very happy and very sad. In fact, in all her eight years, Katy had never felt so mixed-up.

Katy was happy because her mother was going to have a baby.

"Soon," her mom said, patting her big tummy. "The doctor tells me the baby will be born very soon."

But Katy was sad because her grandmother—her most favorite person in the world—was dying.

"Can you believe it?" Grandma said, shaking her white-haired head in disbelief. "The doctor tells me I've precious little time left on this good earth. Well, old girl," she patted Katy's hand, "if that's true, we'd better make the most of it!"

Katy's grandma had always called Katy "old girl." Katy didn't know why, but she knew she liked it.

Now she wondered how her grandma could be so matter-of-fact—almost cheerful—about such bad news.

But then, Katy reminded herself, *Grandma always has been different.*

To begin with, there was the mysterious matter of her age. For as long as Katy could remember, Grandma had claimed to be "thirty-nine and holding." According to the records kept in the old family Bible, Katy figured Grandma was actually eighty-six years old. "Age," Grandma liked to say, "is all in the mind. You're as old as you think you are. Remember that, old girl."

Grandma's eyes were clear blue and sparkly, like two bright marbles, and when she smiled (which was practically all the time), a thousand tiny lines crinkled around them like rays of sunshine.

Grandma's hands were old and gnarled and veiny, like the branches of an old apple tree. But her touch, as she brushed away Katy's bangs when they needed cutting (which was practically all the time), was as soft as the petals of a rose.

She didn't wear much jewelry. Just the wedding ring Grandpa had given her more than half a century ago and a tiny silver cross that had belonged to her younger sister, Mabel, who died of appendicitis when she was only twelve years old. "That was back in the old days before there were wonder drugs like today," Grandma said.

Whenever she talked about Grandpa (who had died before Katy was born) or her sister, Mabel, Grandma always got a faraway look in her eyes. "How I wish you could have known them, old girl," she would say to Katy. "My, how you would make them laugh!"

And Grandma smelled so good, like cinnamon and nutmeg and vanilla. One day Katy caught her in the kitchen, actually using vanilla straight from its little brown bottle as perfume. "When I was a girl about your age," Grandma grinned, "I was desperate to wear perfume and rouge like my older sisters, but Ma forbade me. So I pinched my cheeks 'til they were pink and dabbed vanilla behind my ears. Here," she passed the bottle to Katy, "try a little for yourself."

Grandma knew how to do things no one else did, like make old-fashioned pearl tapioca pudding from scratch. "'Fish eyes in glue,'" Grandma said, standing at the kitchen stove, stirring the sweet, gooey mixture as it bubbled merrily in the glass double boiler. "That's what my brothers used to call my mother's tapioca. Can you imagine? Oh, those boys used to tease poor Ma something terrible!" Grandma laughed and shook her long-handled wooden spoon at Katy. "Now don't you dare go repeating that to your younger brother!"

And everyone looked forward to Saturday mornings, when Grandma made her famous deep-fried buttermilk doughnut holes. It was Katy's job to shake the crisp, warm, fragrant balls in a big brown paper bag filled with powdered sugar. "No one shakes that bag like you, old girl," Grandma would say.

Somehow Grandma always seemed to know the right thing to say.

One Christmas, Katy's favorite gift was a pet hamster. But no one—not even her dad, who usually liked animals—wanted to have anything to do with the furry little creature. "Get that rodent away from me," her dad said gruffly, backing away in alarm when Katy held the hamster up to his face for closer inspection. *"Ee-e-k!"* squealed Katy's mom. "It looks too much like a mouse for me!" As for her little brother—well, all he wanted to do was feed the hamster to his pet snake.

But not Grandma.

"Cute little critter," she said, extending a crooked finger to stroke the hamster's velvet-soft, quivering nose. "Is it a girl or a boy? Have you decided on a name? Why, if you ask me, it looks just like a miniature teddy bear."

Back in the old days, Grandma used to live in town in a big old three-story Victorian house on Main Street. The house had a wide, wraparound front porch with white wicker chairs and a loveseat with faded, flowery cushions. The fancy wooden trim that decorated the outside of the house was called "gingerbread," and in the summertime, Grandma always had lots of hanging baskets with red and pink geraniums. "Peppermint plants," Grandma liked to call them, "to go with my gingerbread house."

But a few years after Grandpa died, Grandma sold the big house and moved in with Katy's family. Ever since Katy could remember, Grandma's bedroom had been upstairs, down the hall and catty-corner from Katy's room. Sometimes, when both their doors were cracked open just right, Katy and Grandma would wave good night to each other from their beds.

But now Grandma was dying.

And not even the arrival of a new baby could take away the deep sadness Katy felt.

What will happen to Grandma when she dies? Katy wondered. *Is there really such a place as heaven? Will we ever get to see each other again?*

One night, Katy was sitting on the family room sofa between her mom and Grandma. The television was turned off, and the three were taking turns feeling the baby's kicks and punches within Katy's mom's big tummy.

"Oo-o-o-! Did you feel that?" Katy's mom grinned. "That was an uppercut, I think. Or maybe a left jab. This little person is a real fighter!"

Grandma smiled. But it was a tired smile and—it seemed to Katy—a sad smile.

"Grandma," Katy said, "are you afraid about dying?"

"Katy!" scolded her mom. "Don't ask such questions."

"Now, now," said Grandma. "Let the girl ask what she likes. It's good to talk."

She cupped her gnarled hands around Katy's.

"Yes, old girl, sometimes I am afraid. I know so much more about life on earth than I do about the new life waiting for me in heaven. But it's perfectly normal to be afraid about things we don't fully understand. It helps when I try to remember that death, in its way, is as natural a part of life as birth. In fact, there's a lot we can learn about death from birth."

Grandma took Katy's hands and placed them on her mom's tummy.

"Think for a moment about this baby here, all cozy and warm, safe and snug in the darkness of your mother's womb," she said.

"Pretend for a moment that this baby can talk. And pretend that you've just told this baby that—whether he liked it or not—a mysterious experience called birth was about to happen to him, and that when it did happen, he would be entering a world unlike anything he could ever imagine.

"Well, I think this baby would probably say something like, 'What? Leave my safe, warm world that I love and know so well and have spent my whole life in for some bright, noisy place I know nothing about? No way!'

"Angry and scared. That's how the baby would most likely feel. Crazy as it may seem, the unborn baby might even have the mistaken idea that what was about to happen to him wasn't birth at all, but *death*—in the sense that everything about life as he knew it was going to come to an abrupt end.

"Because how can you begin to explain to an unborn baby the glorious colors of flowers in spring ... or the magic of dancing rainbows cast by sunlit crystal ... or fireworks on the Fourth of July? How can you explain to an unborn baby the beauty of Mozart being played on the piano ... the sound of laughter ... the taste of a chocolate ice-cream cone with sprinkles ... the smell of fresh-baked cinnamon bread ... and the down softness of a hamster's nose? How can you explain to an unborn baby the way powdered sugar melts to sweetness on the tip of your tongue? The excitement of Christmas Eve? The way it feels to wake up on your birthday morning? The way if feels to be caught in the middle of a family hug, happily squished between your mother and father, like the filling of a sandwich?

"No," Grandma shook her head, "I don't think that what is going to happen to me is death. I like to think of it as *birth*—birth to a new life in a new and wonderful world called heaven. A world more beautiful and full of love and good feelings than anything I've ever known. A world that here and now—like an unborn baby—I can barely begin to imagine."

"But how do you know you're going to heaven, Grandma?" Katy asked.

"Ever since I was a little girl, I've believed in God and Jesus, and in the promises in the Bible," said Grandma. "Ma and Pa taught me that faith was a good and helpful thing to have, and that the Bible was like a guidebook for living. In the Bible it says, *For God loved the world so much that he gave his only son, Jesus, so that whoever believes in him will not die, but will live with him forever.'* That's a promise—and not just for me, but for you, too. And for your mom and dad and brother, and for Grandpa who died already, and for the little baby here who hasn't been born yet. It's God's promise for everyone in the world."

"Where is heaven, Grandma?" Katy asked. "What's it like? Who's there? Will I ever see you again?"

"So many questions, old girl. So many questions …" Thoughtfully, Grandma fingered the tiny silver cross that hung around her neck.

"Heaven," said Grandma, "isn't here on earth, except maybe in our hearts—the way it feels when we love someone and when we know deep-down inside that we are loved back. Then I think we get a glimpse. Take you and me, for instance. Now, there's a bit of heaven, don't you think?"

Katy nodded. Her heart felt like it was going to burst, she loved her grandma so much.

"As human beings here on planet earth," Grandma went on, "God places each of us in time and space for a special purpose. We are born, we live our lives the best we can, and then, when our adventure on earth is over, we die. But heaven is outside time and space. It's like another dimension. We know from the Bible that God our Father has been there always. And Jesus. And all the angels. It is a wonderful place, full of love and peace and forgiveness and joy. *'In heaven,'* the Bible says, *'God will wipe away every tear from every eye.'*

"Personally," said Grandma, "I like to think of heaven as a big birthday party."

Her blues eyes sparkled.

"And I almost forgot the best part. When I get to heaven, I'll get a brand-new body."

Katy and her mom were speechless at this bit of news.

"Now don't you two girls look so surprised," said Grandma, grinning. "This old body you see here isn't the real me, you know. It's just a container, a shell, for my soul, which is the invisible, real me that will go to heaven and live forever. And it's the same for you. Here on earth, our human bodies aren't designed to last forever. Over time they tend to wear out and get old and sick, like mine. Or they meet with a sudden illness or an accident. When this happens and our bodies die, there's a wonderful, mysterious moment when our souls are released to heaven. And once our souls are in heaven, they're wrapped in new bodies—very special bodies that will never get sick, never get old, never feel pain, and will last forever."

"But how?" asked Katy. "How does all that happen? What does it feel like?"

Grandma wrapped her arm around Katy and pulled her close.

"Now that," she said, her blue eyes twinkling, "is a *mystery*. It's a mystery so special that we each have to wait and discover the true meaning of it ourselves, each in our own way, when we die."

The room grew quiet.

No one moved or said a word.

Even the baby was still.

"Oh, Grandma," Katy said, "I'm going to miss you so much when you die."

"And I'll miss you, too, old girl. If there's any way God can keep me up-to-date on what's happening in your life here on earth, I'm sure He will. It helps knowing that we'll all be together again one day in heaven. Remember, that's a *promise*."

She closed her eyes.

"I'm very tired now, dear," she said. "It's best I get myself upstairs and try to get some sleep."

That night, the bedroom doors were cracked open just right so Katy could glimpse Grandma in her bed. The light on her bed stand was on, and she was sitting upright, propped against two plump pillows. Her long white hair hung down around her small shoulders so that from a distance she almost looked like a young girl. Her glasses were low on her nose, and in her hands was a plain black book. She was reading her Bible.

Suddenly, as though sensing Katy's glance, she looked up and smiled. Then she lifted her hand and waved. Katy waved back.

Good night, Grandma, she thought. *I sure do love you.*

And for a moment, she was almost certain she heard Grandma say, "And I love you, too, old girl."

A warm breeze ruffled the curtains, and the sun was streaming through Katy's windows as she awoke. Opening her eyes, she was startled to see her mom sitting at the foot of her bed.

"Grandma ..." her mom's voice was barely a whisper.

Katy's heart felt sick, and she was filled with a sense of dread at what she knew her mom was about to say.

"Grandma died last night." It was hard for her mom to even say the words. "The doctor says her old heart finally just stopped beating. The doctor says she didn't feel any pain—"

Katy watched as her mother's face crumpled with grief, and felt her own throat tighten and her eyes fill with tears. The sense of loss and sadness she felt was so deep and hurt so badly.

"Oh, Mom," Katy cried, wrapping her arms around her mother, "we're going to miss Grandma so much!"

She hugged her mom tightly, and the two of them rocked back and forth, back and forth on the bed, murmuring words of comfort to each other and letting their tears flow.

At the same time, Katy kept thinking of Grandma and her new life in heaven ...

What must it be like, with God and Jesus and all those angels? And Grandpa, and her sister Mabel, and her ma and pa, and all her other sisters and brothers and friends who had died before ... What a grand reunion they must all be having! Like a big birthday party ...

What was it Grandma had said?

Death, in its way, was as natural a part of life as birth.

Though Katy knew she would miss her grandma terribly, she was comforted somehow by this thought.

Yes, it was true Grandma had died. But her soul was forever alive!

Like the baby that would soon be born into this world, Grandma was beginning a new and wonderful love-filled life ... in heaven.

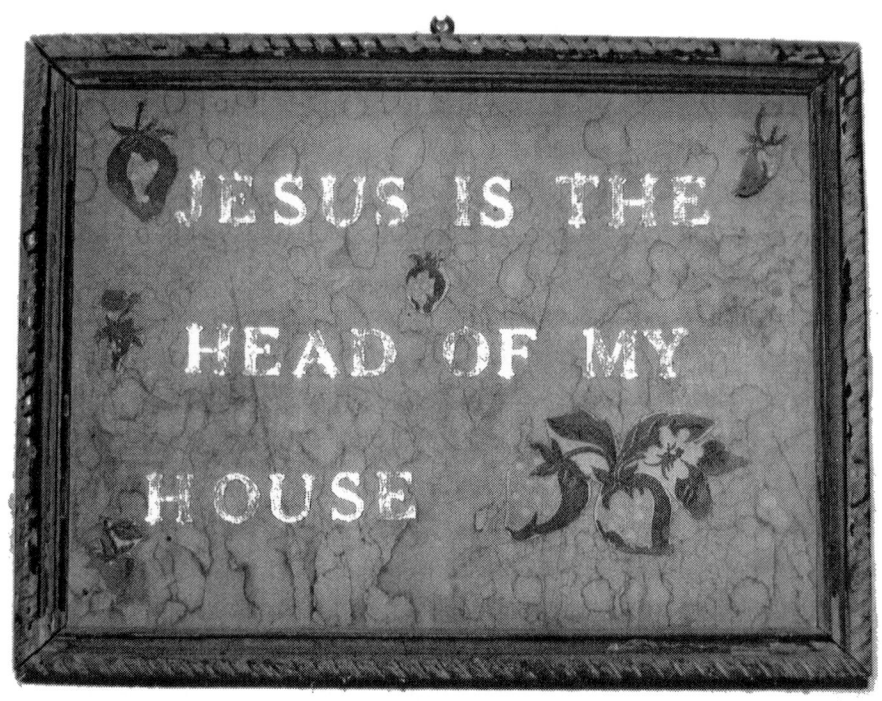

"Jesus Is the Head of My House"

Homecoming

The grizzled old homeless man stood on the corner of the sidewalk on Sixth Avenue. Among the used magazines, tattered clothing, and odds and ends he had spread out to sell, a small plaque caught my eye: "Jesus is the Head of My House." The message was spelled out in silver letters that someone had glued on a five-by-seven-inch scrap of cardboard and then decorated with cutouts of strawberry-patterned wallpaper. The glass was dirty, and the gray paint on the wooden frame was flaking. Maybe the old man had made it himself.

"Is two dollars all right?" I asked, fishing in my purse.

He nodded. I gave him the bills and tucked the plaque in a diaper bag slung over the back of the stroller where my toddler son, Brinck, slept. Then I hurried home.

Even after I cleaned the glass and wiped the frame with a damp cloth, the plaque was dingy. So I hung it on a hook in our closet, where it played peekaboo through the hangers. As the years passed and our children grew, the old plaque moved with us from our first apartment on Horatio Street in Greenwich Village, across town to our co-op on East Eleventh Street, where I hung it on a nail above the laundry tub.

Eventually the day came when Tom and I decided to move to the suburbs, where raising our family would be easier and less expensive. But caught in the Manhattan real-estate crash of 1990, we were unable to sell our co-op—even at a huge loss. So we rented it out to a couple with an option to buy, and leased a rundown house for our family in New Canaan, Connecticut, a leafy suburb with good public schools.

The plaque went on a cobwebby windowsill in the cellar. One winter's morning I found it faceup on the cold cement floor, its glass broken into countless shards.

"Jesus is the Head of My House."

Illuminated by the harsh glare of a naked bulb, the words seemed to mock me. *What house?* I wondered. I missed the city. It had been my dream to live there forever. I hated the place we were renting. Cold in the winter, buggy in summer, it bore the scars of years of tenant neglect. The decades-old harvest-gold paint on the outside was peeling, and the avocado-green shutters were rotting.

Tom's parents had mailed us a handsome personalized doormat for a housewarming present, but I couldn't bring myself to put it out. This was not our home. I was ashamed to welcome any guests. More times than I cared to admit, I'd picked up the phone to ask someone over for coffee and then changed my mind at the last minute.

Sometimes I felt guilty for being unhappy. After all, we had much to be thankful for. We had found a good church. Katy and Brinck were thriving at their new elementary school and making friends. They relished the freedom of a woodsy backyard and loved riding their bikes up and down the block. Tom didn't mind the hour commute to the city on the train—he said it gave him time to catch up on his reading. And we all enjoyed the slower pace of life, the sound of wind in the trees, the cheerful call of black-capped chickadees, and even the sight of deer hungrily nibbling at the rhododendron bushes. (Being tenants, they weren't *our* rhododendron bushes.)

Now I looked at the broken plaque lying on the basement floor. Gingerly I picked up a splinter of glass and tossed it into a plastic trash bucket. I reached for another shard and tossed it. Then another. Finally the glass was all gone, but the framed message was still there: "Jesus is the Head of My House."

And suddenly I got the message. The words spoke with a forcefulness that jolted me out of my gloom. *Of course!* My house was not this leaky, creaky structure built on top of dreary concrete blocks. My house was not our unsold co-op in the city, nor would it be the vintage Dutch colonial we dreamed of someday buying.

My house was my heart. And every day I had the privilege of inviting Jesus to be the head—filling me with His hope, encouragement, guidance, and love. My fingers traced the silver letters. Jesus hadn't been the head of my house for a long time—not since we left the city and moved to Connecticut.

Jesus, I prayed, *I'm so sorry I've shut You out. Please come into my heart and be the head of my house.*

I returned the plaque to its spot on the windowsill. Turning to leave, I noticed a pile of boxes stacked up under the basement stairwell. It took some rummaging, but I found what I was looking for. Running upstairs, I opened the front door and rolled out the doormat. "The Slatterys," it said.

Would we ever sell our co-op? Would we ever own a home again? Somehow those questions didn't seem to matter so much anymore. I headed to the kitchen to phone a friend from church and invite her over for coffee. I was ready to be welcoming.

Thanks to a homeless man, I knew where my home was—and to whom it belonged.

My Secret Garden

It was a blustery December morning, and I sat perched on a stool at the kitchen counter, credit card in hand, in the midst of placing a last-minute phone order for Christmas sweaters for my husband and our two children. While the salesperson put me on hold, I held the phone and its tinny recording of "Frosty the Snowman" away from my ear and gazed out the window.

The pale winter sun glinted off the cars and trucks as they whizzed by our newly purchased house—an old 1929 Dutch colonial on a busy street corner. Our dream home—well, almost. The paint on the white wooden gate that led to our postage stamp-sized backyard was cracked and flaking, and the rusty hinges creaked mournfully in the winter wind. A bright red cardinal fluttered down and perched on the edge of an ancient concrete birdbath filled with frozen water and dead leaves.

I once read that no matter how much a person owns, the average American wants 25 percent more. Everybody, it seems, yearns for *something*—a larger apartment, a new bathroom, an updated kitchen, a fancier car. What I wished for was a bigger backyard. Not only that—more than anything, I dreamed of a *garden*. A *real* garden. You know. The kind of garden lush with flowers, birds, and butterflies.

The salesperson came back on the phone, reviewed my order, and asked if I had any special instructions for the UPS deliveryman.

"Yes," I said. "We live on the corner of a very busy street, and there's no parking in the front. So please tell the deliveryman to *not* use the front door. Tell him to park his truck in the driveway behind the house and come up the back steps. I'll meet him at the back door."

I hung up the phone and looked out the window, hoping to catch a glimpse of the cardinal. But it was gone.

If only I had a bigger, prettier backyard, I sighed with discontent. *If only I had a garden.*

Three days later, the doorbell rang. I went to the back door to greet the UPS man, but no one was there. So I ran to the front door, where the deliveryman stood shivering, his breath coming out in little puffs and his cheeks pink from the winter cold.

"Oh dear," I said as I signed for the package. "You must not have gotten my instructions. I'm sorry you had to walk all the way around to the front. It would have been so much easier for you to come to the back door."

"No problem," he replied. "I started to come up your back steps, but when I saw the gate to your backyard and the garden, I couldn't resist opening it." He smiled sheepishly. "I hope you don't mind. I love gardens—even in winter—and yours is so lovely. It must be so beautiful in the summer. I can just picture it blooming with flowers, butterflies, and so many birds at the birdbath."

I stared dumbly at the package in my hands, not knowing what to say.

A garden! He actually thought our tiny backyard was a garden. And not just any garden. A lovely *garden.*

"Thank you," I mumbled. "You're very kind."

Suddenly, I could hardly wait for spring! I could hardly wait to oil the hinges on the old gate and give it a fresh coat of white paint ... scrub the birdbath and fill it with cool, clear sparkling water ... put on my gardening gloves, grab a trowel, dig in the dirt, and plant lots and lots of pink geraniums, coral impatiens, golden begonias, and purple petunias. Closing my eyes, I could practically smell the black, loamy earth ... feel the warmth of the sun on the back of my neck ... hear the birds singing.

All I had expected from the UPS man was a box of Christmas sweaters. But through His generous and inspired imagination, God had delivered so much more—the garden I'd always dreamed of ...

The garden that had been there all along.

Open my eyes, Lord, to see Your beautiful hidden blessings that are all around me, just waiting to be discovered.

Dad's Flag

On Memorial Day weekend, we invited my seventy-eight-year-old mother to come out from New York City and visit us in the in-law apartment attached to our house in suburban New Canaan, Connecticut. Mom had stayed with us many times before. But this weekend would be different. On this weekend, we would be discussing the possibility of Mom taking the big step of selling her apartment, leaving the city, and moving in with us. Permanently.

My mother enjoyed good health and loved her busy life in Manhattan, but her vision was failing. Age-related macular degeneration had stolen 70 percent of the vision in her left eye, and the retina specialist said it was a condition that would only get worse with time.

Initially, I wasn't so sure that my mother moving in with us was a good idea. We hadn't lived under the same roof since I left home for college. Like many mothers and daughters, we were different in so many ways.

My husband, Tom, on the other hand, was all for the idea of Mom moving in. It was "practical," he said. It was the right thing to do. Plus, over the long term, it would be good for her financially.

On Sunday night, after the dinner dishes were cleared, the three of us lingered at the kitchen table.

"More decaf?" I held the carafe over my mother's cup. She shook her head.

"So, what do you think?" I asked. "About moving in?"

For a long moment, my mother was quiet. And then she sighed. "I like the idea," she said. And then she smiled. "I think—I think it makes sense."

I nodded in agreement. Now that Mom was getting older, I wouldn't worry so much about her if she were next door. We could get right to her if there were an emergency. But still I wondered …

What if it didn't work out? I worried. *What if we didn't get along? What if it turned out Mom didn't like living in our little town? What if we were all making a big mistake?*

That night I tossed and turned, unable to sleep.

Dear God, I prayed, *please reassure me somehow that we're doing the right thing—for all of us.*

The next morning, sunlight streamed through our bedroom window, and a gentle breeze stirred the curtains.

"Hey, Mom!" Ten year-old Brinck called excitedly from downstairs. "Where's my Scout cap?" He was marching with his Cub Scout troop in our town's Memorial Day parade.

Memorial Day!

I jumped out of bed and hastily pulled on my robe. I loved Memorial Day, especially the parade, followed by the ceremonies down at the town cemetery. Indeed, one of the things I loved most about New Canaan—with its wooded ridges and rolling stone walls—was its distinctly New

England character. Our Memorial Day parade was practically identical to the one I had marched in as a freckle-faced Brownie growing up in small-town Medfield, Massachusetts, and for a moment I was overcome by a vivid recollection of that long-ago morning …

Waving a small flag, I marched the mile-long route to the black iron gates of Medfield's cemetery. By the time I got there, my brand-new summer Keds were no longer white, and I had blisters at the back of both heels. For a moment I panicked, lost in the crowd. But then I heard my father calling my name. Holding Dad's hand, I was surprised at how bucolic and parklike the cemetery was—not at all the spooky place I had imagined. Weeping willows dripped their delicate branches in the pond's sparkling waters, and a mother mallard paddled by, followed by her quacking brood of ducklings.

I strained to hear the words of Medfield's oldest surviving World War I veteran, who gave a long speech on an equally ancient public address system that made his voice sound all wobbly—something about "brave men who died so we could live free." The morning sun was hot, and I could feel my bangs getting damp under my brown felt cap. A green mayfly droned lazily by. I tried to concentrate on what the old soldier was saying, but my eyelids grew heavy and my thoughts wandered. Finally the pastor of the Congregational Church offered the closing prayer. At last the time had come for the climactic moment that everyone was waiting for—the twenty-one-gun salute. The young soldiers hoisted their rifles.

Ba-*boom!* … Ba-*boom!* … Ba-*boom!*

Over and over, the shots reverberated, startling babies and sending a flurry of Canadian geese and ducks skyward. After the last echo faded, a trumpeter played taps. Carried by a warm spring breeze, the mournful notes drifted across rows of stone grave markers, many dating back to before the Revolutionary War—some so old the names and dates had been worn away by centuries of sun, wind, rain, and snow. I glanced up at Dad, who never took his eyes off the flag, not for one second. I watched as he brushed a tear from his eye. *Why*, I wondered, *does looking at the flag make Dad cry?* I was too young to understand what patriotism meant. In an effort to comfort my father and to somehow try to absorb whatever it was he was feeling, I wrapped my arms tightly around his ample waist and snuggled as close as I could …

I found Brinck's cap at the back of his closet, leaned over the banister, and tossed it down the stairs. He was sitting on the bottom step, deep in conversation with my mother—something about a flag.

"Hey, Mom," he called up. "Mama B's got a great idea."

"What's that?" I asked, throwing a sweater around my shoulders and heading down the stairs.

"I was just looking at your front door," my mother said. "I think I might have figured out a way for you to hang your dad's flag. You've got a nice overhang for hanging it vertically. All you'd need is a couple of nails …"

Dad's flag.

After his funeral, my mother had surprised me with a neatly folded triangle of red, white, and blue—the flag that had draped his coffin.

"You take this," Mom had said with a sad smile. "You know how patriotic your father was. He'd want you to have it. One day you can pass it on to your children."

The flag had been issued to my mother by Veterans Affairs in recognition of Dad's military service in World War II. That had been more than a decade ago, and for all those years, I had searched in vain for the right spot to hang it.

"Sounds like a good idea to me," said Tom. "Why don't I get the stepladder and we can try to hang the flag before we go?"

"No time," I replied, adjusting the slide on Brinck's blue Scout neckerchief. "If we don't hurry, we'll be late for the parade."

It was only nine o'clock in the morning, but already the sun was high in a cloudless blue sky, and a large crowd had gathered in the center of town. As we found our spots on the curb of Main and Elm Streets, the distant wail of bagpipes and rhythmic boom of big bass drums heralded the parade's approach. First came the Veterans of Foreign Wars, including several young men and women in uniform, who had served in the recent Gulf War. Then came the town council members, the school board, and the Kiwanis Club men, who tossed hard candies into the crowd, sending children scrambling. They were followed by the Hannah

Benedict Carter Chapter of DAR ladies, the town's EMS volunteers, a fleet of antique cars, and "Old Faithful," the fire department's vintage candy apple-red fire truck, crowded with kids waving flags.

"Hooray!" cried the crowd, applauding wildly as each group of marchers passed by.

Finally the Cub Scouts appeared, and there was Brinck, grinning ear to ear and waving his flag. Freckles had popped out across his nose and pink cheeks, and his hair looked damp under his tan cap. With another mile to march, I was glad his sneakers were old and broken in. Finally, the New Canaan Mounted Troop rode by, and the parade was over. The sidewalk crowds spilled onto Main Street, and everyone headed for the town cemetery for the Memorial Day ceremonies.

"Shall we walk down to the cemetery?"

Tom took my hand.

"No," I said. "Not this year. Let's round up Mom and the kids and go home and hang Dad's flag."

"Are you sure?" asked Tom. "You always like the ceremonies—especially the twenty-one-gun salute."

I nodded. "I'm sure. I can't explain it exactly, but I've just got the strangest feeling that we need to get home and put out the flag."

Back home, Mom and I held the stepladder while Tom hammered two nails into the overhang above the front door. In less than five minutes, the job was done.

"C'mon." I took Mom's hand. "Let's go out to the sidewalk to get a good look."

Together we walked down the path to the front gate, where we stopped and turned to look back at the house. The flag was magnificent. It was just the right size for the doorway. Its brilliant red and white stripes and stars on a field of navy blue stirred grandly in the gentle spring breeze.

Dad's flag had finally found a home.

Suddenly, in the distance, drifting up from the cemetery, we heard what sounded like rolling thunder.

Ba-*boom!* ... Ba-*boom!* ... Ba-*boom!*

The twenty-one-gun salute.

Mom's lower lip started to quiver, and I wrapped my arm around her shoulder. Gazing at the flag and listening to the sound of the guns, it was as though Dad were standing right there with us. I could almost sense the bighearted warmth of his presence, and I knew Mom did too.

If we'd gone to the cemetery, we would have totally missed this moment together, I thought. *What incredible timing!*

God's timing.

As the echo of the last gunshot faded, I heard the whisper of His familiar, reassuring voice in my heart.

Don't worry. You and your mom are both doing the right thing. You're both where you're supposed to be. It won't always be easy. There will be ups and downs. But I will be with you.

Not only had Dad's flag found a home.

Mom was home too.

Mom and Dad, July, 1944, Miami, Florida

The Power of Human Kindness

When our son was young, there was a bully in his fifth-grade class who mostly picked on little kids. But one day he chose our robust son as the object of his scorn. It wasn't the physical aspect of being bullied that bothered Brinck. He was big enough in stature to take care of himself. It was the boy's inexplicable cruelty that troubled him most.

"Mom," he asked, "why do people hurt other people?"

How to respond to such a big question from our tenderhearted son? A variety of possible answers ran through my mind. *People are not perfect ... Sometimes they lash out and hurt others because they are scared ... or sad ... or sick ...*

And then I remembered my dog Roxie.

When I was a little girl, I explained to Brinck, I had a beautiful fawn boxer with a black mask and white paws. We got her from a family who lived down the street and had to move away overseas. Although Roxie was a young boxer, no more than two years old, we were her third family. We didn't know anything about her first home. But we did know that the family we got her from often went away on long trips, and when they did, they kept Roxie locked up in their cold, dark basement. Roxie was a very friendly boxer and didn't like being left alone. She panicked and barked and scratched at the basement door. Sometimes she scratched the door so hard that her paws bled.

A few weeks after Roxie came to live with us, I was in my bedroom packing for a family vacation. The moment Roxie saw my open suitcase, she growled, looked at me with suspicious, frightened eyes, and bolted from the room. It took my father an hour to catch her, and we nearly missed the plane. I loved Roxie, and it hurt my feelings that she would growl at me and run away.

"Why would Roxie do such a thing?" I asked my father on the way to the airport. "Does it mean she isn't happy in her new home? Does it mean she doesn't like me?"

He explained that Roxie behaved the way she did because she was afraid. She had been hurt by her previous owners, he said, and she didn't want to be hurt again.

For a long moment, Brinck was silent. I could almost hear him thinking.

"So when people hurt each other, it's because they've been hurt, too?" he asked.

"Yes," I nodded.

I wished I could tell our son that Roxie eventually got over her fear of suitcases, but she did not. Still, we loved her, and she loved us back. She was a good dog and lived a long life.

Today I am the owner of a roly-poly pug named Max, whose story is very different from Roxie's. Max came to live with us when he was a fluffy little puppy, just ten weeks old. A few days after his arrival, I was outside teaching Max how to walk with a leash, when I bumped into my friend Gail. With her houseful of three spirited West Highland terriers, Gail was one of the biggest dog lovers I'd ever known. She was also a pastor at our local church.

"O-o-o-o-o!" she exclaimed. "What a cute little puppy!" She scooped Max up and held him close to her cheek—a warm wiggly ball of snuffly pug kisses. "Would it be all right if I said a prayer for him?" she asked.

"Okay," I agreed, although I had never heard of praying for a dog before—especially on a public sidewalk with pedestrians and cars passing by.

Gail cradled her hands around Max's little head. She gently stroked his velvety black ears, and he happily looked up at her with his wrinkly brow and trusting black eyes.

Happy Max amongst the daffodils

"Lord Jesus," she prayed, "thank You for bringing this precious little puppy into my friend's life. Help her provide Max with a safe, happy home—and may he be a dog that only knows human kindness. Amen."

May he be a dog that only knows human kindness, I thought. What a *beautiful* prayer!

Not a day goes by that I don't think of Gail's words, and I'm grateful to report that Max is, indeed, a dog that has been blessed to only know human kindness. As a result, he is the happiest, roly-poliest pug I know. When Max sees an open suitcase, he doesn't growl and run away. Instead, he jumps in, rolls on his back, sticks out his pink tongue, and waits for me to tickle his tummy. And there's nothing that makes him happier than when his boy Brinck—now a grown man and tenderhearted as ever—comes home to visit.

Why do people hurt other people?

People are not perfect, it is true. But like it says in the Bible, we can begin to make a difference by reaching out to others with human love and kindness. And we can remember to pray for each other. It's amazing what kindness and prayer can do—not only for puppies, but people too.

Important Things: In Memoriam, September 11, 2001

It was a September morning like any other. The air was still summer warm. The sky was a brilliant robin's egg blue. I stepped onto the 8:25 a.m. Metro North commuter train, headed toward my office at *Guideposts* magazine on Thirty-Fourth Street in New York City.

"Excuse me." I squeezed between a young woman wearing earphones who was thumbing through the color photo-filled pages of *Star Magazine* and a middle-aged gray-bearded man reading the *New York Times*.

Drat. The dreaded middle seat. Oh well, at least I don't have to stand.

I put on my sunglasses and folded my arms tightly across my chest, as though doing so might somehow make me not only smaller but also invisible. Before closing my eyes, I sneaked glances at the headlines in my seatmates' reading material—a microcosm of everyday life in twenty-first-century America. On my left, in *Star*, there was the insatiable culture of celebrity ("Look Who's Got Cellulite!"). On my right, in the *New York Times*, bitter partisan politics ("Campaigning for Mayor: City Voters Have Heard It All"). Oozing from the pages of both—as well as from the jokes told the night before on the late-night-TV talk shows—was the prevailing tone of world-weary, been there-done that, above-it-all irony.

I'd just dozed off when someone's cell phone chirped—followed by another, and then another. Passengers began speaking in hushed, urgent tones, something about one of the World Trade Center's twin towers being hit by a plane. Not a small private plane. A big commercial airliner.

How awful, I thought. *What a terrible accident.*

Several minutes passed, and a second shrill chorus of cell phones announced a second strike.

This was no accident. We were being attacked.

The bearded man next to me became agitated as he punched the buttons on his cell phone, to no avail. "My staff is on the eighty-sixth floor of tower one," he said. "My God, I hope they're all right."

As the train rounded the bend north of 125th Street, passengers across the aisle left their seats to peer out the train's west windows at the terrifying spectacle of the towers burning.

At Grand Central Station, I wedged myself into the crowd at the Hudson News kiosk, transfixed by the horrifying images on the elevated Fox News TV monitors. Fiery orange explosions. People jumping from the towers. Skirts billowing. A man and woman holding hands as they plummeted.

This can't be happening.

Walking south on Fifth Avenue, I watched aghast as the blue sky filled with black smoke hemorrhaging from ugly gashes in both towers. At street level, there was the surreal sensation of being in a 1950s' Japanese horror movie. People with radios and cell phones pressed to their ears shouted breaking news.

"They've hit the Pentagon!"

"There's a plane headed for the White House!"

At the office, I frantically tried to phone my husband, Tom, who had driven into Manhattan earlier in the morning for a breakfast meeting with a client somewhere in the city … *But where exactly? Downtown? Uptown? If only I had asked!* I tried to call Katy at her New York University dorm downtown on Greenwich Street. I tried to call my sister in her classroom at Middle School 131 in downtown Chinatown, where she taught sixth-grade science. But none of their cell phones were working.

"Did you hear?" a young, ashen-faced staffer cried out from her office across the hall. "The south tower has fallen!"

I phoned my mother back at our house in New Canaan, Connecticut, and told her not to worry. I phoned my friend Alison and told her I couldn't get in touch with Tom, Katy, or my sister, that they were all downtown, and would she please pray?

"Of course," she replied. "Oh, my God, Kitty. Are you near a television? The north tower is falling …"

My desk phone rang. It was Tom. He was safe. I sobbed with relief. His breakfast meeting had not been downtown but just five blocks away, on Thirty-Ninth Street at the Williams Club, where Tom, an alumnus of Williams College, was a member. We agreed to meet there, where the staff was busy setting up phone banks and tables with bottled water and emergency provisions.

As the morning dragged on, men and women covered in white dust, looking like ghosts, staggered up the steps and through the door. Survivors from the horror downtown, they had walked the four miles to the Williams Club in shock.

Once we finally got through to Katy and my sister and made sure they were safe, and called my mother and our son Brinck at his high school to reassure them that we were all okay, Tom and I headed for home via the West Side Highway. It was three o'clock in the afternoon. Across from us on the southbound lane, an endless convoy of ambulances and emergency vehicles from the northern suburbs, including New Canaan, moved toward what the newscaster on the radio was calling "Ground Zero." I turned around in my seat and looked south, where a dismal, dirty gray cloud filled the empty space where the twin towers had stood. It seemed impossible that they were gone. National Guardsmen, armed with rifles and wearing camouflage uniforms and black boots, stood at the Henry Hudson Bridge tollgates and inspected our car before letting us pass.

When we finally made it home, Tom and I pulled my father's flag—the flag that had covered Dad's casket when he died—out from the darkness of the closet and hung it over the front door. Across the street and next door, our neighbors had put out their flags, too.

As I stood looking at the flag, I remembered how as a teenager, my father's patriotism had embarrassed me. At high school football games, I wanted to hide when he placed his right hand over his heart and lustily bellowed every word to "The Star-Spangled Banner." Back then, my father's old-fashioned, unapologetic patriotism seemed not only corny but irrelevant. Forged by the fires of adversity and sacrifice, his patriotism was the birthright of a different generation—the Greatest Generation—surely something that could never burn in my privileged baby boomer's heart.

Until now.

The two towers were not all that fell on that awful day. If only for a moment, all that was trivial about everyday American life fell away, too. The culture of celebrity. Partisan politics. Irony. All were unmasked as the cheap, shallow, frivolous imposters that they were.

Rising out of the ruins, all that remained standing were the important things. Faith. Family. Friends. Freedom. Essential and enduring, they offered meaning and hope to a nation and people suffering incalculable heartache and loss.

Now, I thought, *is the time to say, "I love you." Now is the time to say, "I'm sorry." Now is the time to say, "Thank you." Now is the time to make peace with God. Now is the time. Tomorrow may be too late.*

On September 11, 2001, it was all so clear.

Waiting for the Call

It's eleven o'clock on Wednesday night. I am waiting for our son, Brinck's, midweek call home from boarding school. It's Wednesday night, and he's supposed to call. That's our agreement. *So why hasn't he called?* I try to chase away the worrisome thoughts gathering on the horizon of my mind like menacing black storm clouds.

Eleven-fifteen. Still no call. Is he not calling because there's something he doesn't want to tell us? Has he had a disappointment? Is there bad news? Did he do poorly on a test? Did he lose his wrestling match? Is he unhappy? Sick?

Eleven-thirty. Time for lights-out in Brinck's dorm. I reach up and turn out the lamp on my bed stand, but I can't sleep. I am disappointed, a little bit angry, and most of all, *anxious*. If only I could stop worrying. St. Andrew's is a very good school, not too far away. We see Brinck every weekend. Still, the unwelcome, troublesome worries go 'round and 'round and 'round in my head.

"Tom?" The sleeping form beside me stirs.

"Huh."

"It's eleven-thirty."

"Don't worry. He'll call."

Eleven-thirty-five. The green digits glow ominously in the dark.

Eleven-forty.

Eleven-forty-five. The room is silent. No chance he'll call now. It's way too late. There's nothing for me to do but go to sleep and look forward to tomorrow, when the morning sun will chase the nagging

Brinck, junior year of high school

disappointment and worry away. The pillow feels so cool and soft. I close my eyes … And then, a peculiar thought.

God? Is it possible that You wait for me to come to You in prayer the way I wait for my son's call? When I come to You in prayer, does it make You happy—the way it makes me so happy when our son calls? Could You really love me that much?

Barely has the thought taken shape in my mind when God answers.

Yes, *I wait to hear from you the same way you wait to hear from your son.* Yes, *I love you that much—and more. Trust me. And stop worrying. I know your concerns. And I'm watching over your son.*

God's *yes* illuminates the darkness, chasing away my fear and filling me with hope. If only for a moment, I stop worrying.

And suddenly—the phone rings.

"Mom?"

"Is everything all right?"

"Everything's fine. Sorry it's so late, but choir rehearsal ran long. I hope I didn't wake you. I know it's Wednesday, and I know you and Dad expect me to call."

"Oh, Brinck," I say, trying to not let him hear the flood of relief that washes over me like a cleansing rain. "It's so good to hear your voice! There's no need to be sorry. It's never too late to call. Never."

Thank You, Lord, for Your loving patience! Forgive me when I keep You waiting! Thank You that You're always so happy to hear from me, and that it's never too late to reach out to You through prayer.

Dear God: Help! An Anxious Mother's Conversation with God

Dear God,

I come to You today desperately seeking peace. I can't take being emotionally jerked around by the ups and downs of my teenage son's life. He's up, I'm up. He's down, I'm down. It's a roller-coaster ride I don't want to be on. But for some inexplicable reason, I've strapped myself in, and I can't get off.

You know my son, God. He's such a good kid—no, a *great* kid—with strengths and weaknesses. Just like me, he is a work in progress. But sometimes I am so scared and anxious about his future, Lord. I don't always have confidence in his ability to make the right decisions and do the right thing. I can't control him. So how can I ever know peace?

You know about the many sleepless nights I toss and turn in the darkness, consumed with runaway worry. The anxiety is unbearable. I can't go on like this, Lord. Please talk to me. How am I to get through these teenage years?

Lord?

My grace is sufficient for you.

Lord, is that really You? I've heard those words—that promise—before. It's in the Bible. But I don't understand. What does it mean?

It means I will help you. There will be more problems, conflicts, trouble, and disappointments in your son's life. But by My grace, he—and you—will get through them. There will be many successes and happy surprises in your son's life, too.

Okay, then. So we'll get by. The future won't be more than we can bear. But I'm still his mother. And I'm still stuck on this runaway roller coaster of worry. How do I ever get off? What is it You want me to *do*?

Give your son to Me.

No. I won't.

Give him to Me.

No. I can't.

Give him to Me.

No. *I don't want to!*

You say you want peace. Listen to Me. Deep down inside, you know that the reason you cannot stop worrying about your son is because in his youth and imperfect humanness he will surely have troubles. Put your confidence in Me. *Trust* Me. *Have confidence in* Me *and entrust* Me *with your son. Then you will know peace. Remember the story of Abraham and Isaac? You must give Me your son, with absolute faith, trusting the way Abraham trusted when he gave Me Isaac.*

All right then. I'll give him to You. Why shouldn't I? You are the God of the whole universe. You are the one true God, whose very nature is good and loving. So why shouldn't I trust You? Take my son. Take him!

Deep down inside, you know he never truly belonged to you. You've enjoyed him all these years as a blessing from Me to you, on loan. I have trusted you with him, and you have loved him and done the best you can. Now, in faith, at My request, you have returned him to Me. This is good, because he belongs to Me. He has always belonged to Me. I have known and loved him since before he was born. My angels watch over him. I have counted every hair on his head, and all his days are numbered and written in My Book of Life.

Yes, Lord. My son belongs to You. In his baptism, he was sealed with Your Holy Spirit and marked as Christ's own forever. He is becoming a man. My role as his human parent must recede, while your role as his perfect parent increases. But still I am his mother. In my weakness, still I will worry. And still I will pray.

And I will hear you.

Prayer for a Teenage Son

Thank You, Lord, for Your perfect love for my son!
Protect him from evil, Lord. Guide him to
goodness and wholeness and truth.
Indwell him. Inspire him. Have mercy on him. Forgive him.
Be patient with him. Comfort him. Heal him.
Be close to him in his waking and in his sleep,
in the classroom and on the playing fields,
and with his teachers, coaches, and friends.
Keep talking to him, Lord.
Come crashing into his heart, and give him a
vivid sense of Your reality and love,
and of Your unique, exciting purposes for
his life here on planet earth.
Help him grow up to be a good and godly man.
And help me too. When I start to get anxious
and controlling, help me to let go,
get out of Your way, and watch in faith and awe as
You do Your perfect work in my son's life.
Align my will with Your will, Lord.
Help me trust You more and be the kind of
mother that You want me to be.

How to Say Good-Bye to Worry

I've always been a worrier.

When I was little, we had a small ceramic ashtray on our coffee table that was decorated with a picture of a tidy little house with a red roof, white-picket fence, and these words: "Don't worry. It may never happen."

Oh, but I did. Worry, that is. About everything. A lot.

One day when I was ten years old, I noticed a new freckle on my nose. I'd recently read in *Reader's Digest* about something called skin cancer. *What if I had skin cancer too?* I worried. When I told my mother about my fears and she told me to stop being such a "worry wart," I worried that all my worrying was going to give me warts!

Sometimes when I was busy at school or playing with friends or lost in a good book, worry would leave me alone. But it always returned—chronic, vague, and menacing. On the sunniest days, it lurked inside me like a storm cloud, threatening to steal my joy.

As I grew older, I began to see how worry, for me, was more than a bad habit. It was the way I was emotionally and psychologically wired. Worry was my futile way of trying to *control the uncontrollable.* And if I was honest, I had to admit that my chronic worry revealed a certain *lack of trust,* not only toward myself and others but also toward God. If I truly believed in a loving, trustworthy God, why should I worry about anything?

One night I tossed and turned in bed, waiting for our teenage son to come home from a party. I glanced at the illuminated numbers on the clock on my bed stand and felt a surge of anxiety. He was fifteen minutes past his curfew. Lying there in the dark, alone with my racing thoughts, I quickly became convinced that our son was:

1. Being pulled over by a policeman for some unthinkable infraction of the law that would ruin his life forever …

2. Being loaded into an ambulance, sirens wailing, lights flashing, heading for the hospital, or …

3. The Mother of All Fears (and, I suspect, the fear of all mothers): *lying somewhere in a ditch.*

This was not just any ditch. No, this ditch was a bottomless black hole that not only contained my fifteen-minutes-past-his-curfew son but also contained every deepest, darkest fear I ever had—or ever would have—about anyone or anything. Over the years, I came to think of it as the "worry ditch." And once I fell into the worry ditch, it was next to impossible to climb out.

I should mention that throughout this fevered episode of high anxiety, my husband, Tom (*not* a worrier), was beside me slumbering peacefully. He was also snoring. I was about to poke him in the ribs to share my mental distress (and stop his snoring) when I was struck with a new insight as to *why* I spent so much time worrying: *Worrying gave me a false sense that I was "doing something" about a problem, when in fact, I was actually wasting valuable mental and emotional energy and accomplishing nothing!*

For me, worrying served as a subversive "win-win" mental mind game. If my worst fear *did not* come true, there was the promise of a pleasurable rush of relief. (Upon hearing the sound of my son's footsteps coming up the stairs, I would be able to think: *Thank God! He's home safe and sound!*) On the other hand, if my worst fear *did* come true (Officer: "Mrs. Slattery, we're so sorry to inform you that we have found your son in a ditch."), I would at least have the satisfaction—hollow, impoverished, and pitiful as such satisfaction might be—of being able to say, "*See, I was right. I knew all along this would happen!*"

So what, as a chronic worrier, was I to do?

The Bible has a lot to say about worry.

In Matthew's gospel, Jesus gets right to the point. "'Do not worry,' He says. '"Can any one of you by worrying add a single hour to your life? ... So *do not worry*'" (Matthew 6:25–27, 31, KJV). It's worth noting that the apostle Paul does *not* encourage us to "Worry without ceasing." Instead, he writes, "*Pray* without ceasing." Prayer is a positive action for the worrier. Indeed, it could be said that prayer is both the opposite and antidote to worry.

I have a friend who likens her tendency to worry to the "thorn" that, despite Saint Paul's fervent prayers that it be removed, afflicted the apostle throughout his life. (See 2 Corinthians 12:6–8) "When I find myself worrying," she says, "I use it as a reminder of how much I need God." On her nightstand she keeps a plaque that reads: "Stop worrying and go to sleep. I'll be up all night anyway. Love, God."

So the next time you find yourself tossing and turning in the middle of the night, take a deep breath and remember:

- Worrying is a waste of valuable time and accomplishes nothing!

- God, who loves you and knows what is best for you, has told you not to worry!

- Use worry as an opportunity to draw you closer to God.

- God loves you and knows your concerns—even better than you do! In other words, God knows what He's doing. He's God.

- The Bible says that God's ways are not our ways and His timing is not our timing. This is a profound truth that can offer tremendous relief from worry. (See Isaiah 55:8–9 and 2 Peter 3:7–9.)

- Give your worries to God in *prayer*. Remember, He's up all night anyway!

Finally, here are my favorite Bible verses for when I'm feeling worried. I hope you find them comforting too!

Cast your cares on the LORD and he will sustain you (Psalms 55:22).

Therefore I tell you, do not worry about your life, what you will eat or drink; or about your body, what you will wear. Is not life more important than food, and the body more important than clothes? Look at the birds of the air; they do not sow or reap or store away in barns, and yet your heavenly Father feeds them. Are you not much more valuable than they? Who of you by worrying can add a single hour to his life? ... So do not worry ... (Matthew 6:25–27, 31).

Do not let your hearts be troubled. Trust in God; trust also in me (John 14:1).

Peace I leave with you; my peace I give you. I do not give to you as the world gives. Do not let your hearts be troubled and do not be afraid (John 14:27).

Do not be anxious about anything, but in everything, by prayer and petition, with thanksgiving, present your requests to God. And the peace of God, which transcends all understanding, will guard your hearts and your minds in Christ Jesus (Philippians 4:6–7).

Cast all your anxiety on him because he cares for you (1 Peter 5:7).

Out of Empty Nest Valley

Tom and me ... empty nesters!

To our left, the Santa Lucia Mountains jutted into the cornflower-blue western sky. To our right, the Pinnacles Mountains rose likewise into the cloudless east. And rushing alongside our tour bus windows in a blur of emerald, teal, mint, and Kelly green was the verdant, flat patchwork quilt of California's Salinas Valley.

The tour guide's microphone crackled with upbeat commentary.

"Nestled between two mountain ranges, the Salinas Valley offers the perfect soil and climate for lettuce, asparagus, cabbage, tomatoes, carrots, kale, broccoli, and grapes," he said. "We call it America's salad bowl."

Tourists on the bus chuckled.

Not me. I reached for a tissue to dab my eyes and blow my nose. Sitting next to me, my husband, Tom, rolled his eyes as if to say, "Here we go again." In a gesture of understanding, he reached for my hand. But I pulled away and glumly turned my face to the window.

I'd read about "empty nest syndrome" in magazines, listened to older friends talk about it, but never had experienced it firsthand—until now.

Only two weeks earlier, Tom and I had said good-bye to our son and daughter as they went off to college. Now, with both children gone, it felt more like two years. Although the hot California sun blazed in the September sky and the tour guide told us that it was a seasonable (for California) eighty-two degrees outside, a cold lonely wind swept through my heart.

It wasn't that I had too much time on my hands. With two hefty tuitions to pay, I was working harder than ever. Instead of feeling down in the dumps, I should be grateful and happy for the opportunity to join Tom on his business trip to California. After all, wasn't this exactly the sort of grown-up vacation getaway we had dreamed of for so many years?

I pressed my forehead harder against the cold glass window, and vivid memories rushed through my mind, fast as the passing scenery ...

Lullabies ... the scent of baby powder ... bedtime prayers ... birthday parties ... Christmas mornings ... hamsters ... tricycles ... training wheels ... skinned knees ... big hugs ... hamster babies ... Girl Scout cookies ... Cub Scout meetings ... more hamster babies! ... *My Little Ponies* ... *Teenage Mutant Ninja Turtles* ... hamster funerals ... lemonade stands ... Christmas pageants ... ballet recitals ... piano lessons ... science projects ... slumber parties ... football games ... first dates ... driving lessons ... high school proms ... graduations ...

Each tender memory was like a little death, each deserving its own time for grieving. But it was too much loss to process. *Too much change, too fast!*

I tried to comfort myself with the knowledge that Katy and Brinck were not only where they wanted to be but where they *should* be. This was a happy, exciting time in their young lives, a season of new discoveries, challenges, and growth. Their new school communities provided safe places where they could try their wings and soar.

But I didn't want to let go! I missed being involved in the intimate, day-to-day details of my children's lives. For so many years, I had been responsible for their safety, for their wellness, and for a wholesome home environment. I watched what they ate, what books they read, what TV programs they watched, and who their friends were.

Now, it somehow didn't feel right not knowing what they'd had for breakfast, if they were dressed warmly enough, what books they were reading, who their friends were, what recent experience had caused them to think more deeply or laugh or—perish the thought!—cry. Let's face it. I didn't like the fact I no longer had *control* over these things. I tried to chase away anxious thoughts about the inevitable youthful mistakes and hurts they would experience—all part of being human and growing up, but still so painful.

Please, God, keep our children safe. Help their mistakes be learning experiences—the kind of life lessons that ultimately serve to build character.

And then there was Tom. Who was this stranger sitting next to me? Without the daily details of our children's lives to discuss, what exactly was our marriage supposed to be about? I think what scared me even more than life apart from our kids was the unknown prospect of our new empty-nest life together.

It's as though our children are off dancing on the mountaintops, I thought. *While Tom and I are left behind, stuck in the valley.*

My thoughts were interrupted by the crackling microphone.

"Pretty as those mountaintops are, folks," the tour guide said, "remember this: *It's down in the valley where everything grows.*"

Again, Tom reached for my hand.

Don't worry, I heard God's gentle whisper in my heart. *I'll watch over your children. The time has come for you and Tom to move on.*

I took my husband's hand and gripped it tightly.

God had brought us safely this far. Surely, with His help, new discoveries, challenges, and growth were waiting for us, too … just around the bend.

Thank You, Lord, for change! I accept your challenge to grow.

Mom & Dad, out for a night dancing, 1948

Tom and me… dancing!

Photo credit: www.ScottJonesPhotography.com

The Dancing Lesson

Over the years, my mother had grown very fond of my husband, Tom. She said that he was a good man and that I was lucky to have "found him."

"Well, we sort of found *each other*," I corrected her. It was a small thing, but I couldn't let it go. *Why was I always so eager to pick a fight?* I thought. My prickly churlishness was like a bad habit.

"You know, Kitty," she went on, ignoring my remark, "it may not always seem like it, but these are the best years of your lives. You two kids should do everything you can to make the most of them."

"Uh-huh," I replied, only half-listening. *Why did she insist on calling us "kids"?* And this wasn't the first time she had told me that these were "the best years of our lives." *Why did she keep on repeating the same thing over and over? As far as I could see, each year of married life was pretty much like the other …*

Then the day came when *our* "kids" went off to college. They hadn't been gone more than a month when Tom surprised me by saying how he thought it might be fun for the two of us—after so many years—to finally learn how to dance.

Unlike my parents, dancing had never played a significant role in our relationship. Sure, we could do a primitive slow dance, and we could hold our own in a stand-apart fast dance. But we didn't know how to twirl to a waltz, swivel our hips to a Latin beat, or spin and swing to the jitterbug. Okay. I'll admit it. After nearly twenty-five years of marriage, we still didn't know how to *dance*. At weddings and dinner dances, it wasn't much fun to be left sitting at the table when everyone else was up on the dance floor.

So I agreed. We would take dancing lessons.

When I told my mother, her eyes lit up.

"Dancing lessons!" she cried. "What a *wonderful* idea! You two kids are going to *love* dancing."

"Aw, Mom," I said, "I don't know. We're not like you and Dad."

I remembered my parents gliding across the kitchen floor to the sweet strains of Benny Goodman and Peter Duchin, finishing with a dramatic dip. My mother would look up at my father with dreamy eyes and sigh, "Oh, *John*." And he would respond in his best Ralph Kramden *Honeymooners* voice, "Baby, you're the greatest!"

I also remembered how back in seventh grade, my mother had signed me up for Sunday night cotillion classes. I was shy, awkward, and clumsy. I blamed it on the boys. Their palms were sweaty. They stepped on my toes. Plus, they were way too short. Our instructor was an elegant older gentleman with slicked-back pewter hair and a pencil moustache, who tried his best to teach the box step to the creaky beat of Jimmy Gilmer and Fireballs' "Sugar Shack." All I wanted to do was tear off my short white gloves and race home in time to see the Beatles sing "I Wanna Hold Your Hand" on the *Ed Sullivan Show*.

At our first dancing lesson, I placed my left hand on Tom's shoulder and extended my right arm. He, in turn, rested his right hand on the small of my back and placed his left hand in mine. So far, so good …

When suddenly, inexplicably, I felt as though I was back in seventh grade—shy and insecure about being so close to this strange boy. My heart pounded, and my palms were sweaty. *If only I had my little white gloves!*

Our instructor was an upbeat middle-aged man named Charlie, who wore a pale blue golf shirt, navy blazer, and comfortable leather loafers. Light as a feather, he moved smoothly alongside us, demonstrating a supposedly simple waltz step. But for some reason, I found it impossible to simultaneously listen to Charlie's instructions *and* the music while moving. When he opened his mouth, his voice sounded like the muted trumpet "*Wah-wah-wah*" of the teacher in the animated *Peanuts* cartoons. No matter how hard I tried to concentrate, I was unable to make my feet do what they were supposed to do.

"Left-two-three. Right-two-three ..." Charlie chanted.

But whose left? Whose right? Tom's or mine?

"Back-two-three. Forward-two-three ..."

Stiff and awkward, I felt like an idiot. Plus, I was getting hot. I stuck out my lower lip and blew a blast of cool air under my bangs. This dancing was hard work. Why, it was practically a *sport!*

At the end of the class, Charlie handed Tom a CD that included a mix of music for slow dancing, the cha-cha, the waltz, and the jitterbug. "See you next week." He waved good-bye. "And remember to practice!"

In the car on the way home, I took off my shoes and massaged my aching toes.

"So what do you think?" I asked Tom.

"I think you need to get yourself a more comfortable pair of shoes," he said.

After dinner, he pushed aside the glass-topped coffee table and overstuffed chair in the sunroom to create a space for dancing. It wasn't a very large space, but the floor was hardwood, and it was where the CD player was located. For the next two nights, we practiced. First the slow dance, then the cha-cha, the waltz, and the jitterbug.

With every dance, I thought I kept the beat better than Tom. And I told him so, which, upon seeing his slightly hurt expression, I immediately regretted.

So, which is more important? I wondered as we lurched past the sofa and potted plants. *Keeping the beat or following Tom's lead? I don't like following. And why should I follow anyway? Tom doesn't know any more about dancing than I do.*

And then, on our third night practicing, a strange thing happened.

For a moment, I forgot about keeping the beat, or watching my feet, or paying attention to whether I was leading or following. I simply closed my eyes and relaxed. It was just the two of us, lost in the music ...

Dancing.

"Hey," Tom whispered. "You're good."

"No," I said. "It's you."

I remembered how I had felt when we first met—the strong attraction, the blissful lightheadedness. It was all so ... *romantic.*

No wonder my parents enjoyed dancing so much, I thought.

The next morning, I bumped into my mother outside her back door, where she was waiting for a friend to pick her up to go to the Ladies' Guild meeting at church. While her poor vision from age-related macular degeneration prevented her from working on the group's fundraising crafts projects, the women insisted that she come to the meetings anyway. They said they enjoyed her company. They also enjoyed her plates of fresh-baked homemade chocolate cake and banana bread.

"So how are the dancing lessons going?" she asked.

"So far, so good," I said.

"Glad to hear it. Are you practicing?"

I nodded. "Every night. In the sunroom."

"Good," she said. "It's the practicing that makes all the difference."

"That's exactly what our instructor told us," I said.

"Sounds like you have a good teacher."

She smiled, and her eyes got a faraway look. I knew what was coming next.

"Remember, Kitty," she said, "it may not always seem like it, but these are the best years of your lives. You two kids should do everything you can to make the most of them."

For some reason, it didn't bother me so much that she called us "kids." And it didn't matter that she had told me that these were "the best years of our lives" more times than I could remember.

A car horn sounded from the driveway.

"There's my ride," she said.

I watched as she made her way down the back steps. Slender and erect, she wore a fashionable leopard-print silk scarf draped around her neck, and a wide black belt cinched her narrow waist. Her auburn hair was coiffed in the same short, fluffy, teased 'do she had worn back when I was in high school. As she descended the concrete stairs, she gripped the white wooden railing tightly, and her lips moved slightly as she counted each step, "eight … nine … ten …" until she safely stepped onto the driveway. Before getting into her friend's car, she turned and waved.

I knew she couldn't see me, but I waved back anyhow.

A bittersweet pang tugged at my heart as I suddenly grasped the hard-earned wisdom of what my widowed mother—a woman acquainted with loss—had been trying for so long to tell me: *Tom and I would not have each other forever.* Soon enough, the day would come when one of us would be gone. If only for the simple fact that we were together, each day was a gift to be appreciated, savored, and lived to the fullest, with or without dancing.

My mother was right.

These *were* the best years of our lives.

New Year's Reflection on "Perfection"

Can you believe it? Another New Year. Time for setting goals and making resolutions. For me, that means time to start trying to lose five pounds. Time to start trying to set aside a regular quiet time. Time to start trying to worry less and pray more ... Hold on a minute. These are exactly the same resolutions I had last year!

As we begin this New Year—each with our own desires for self-improvement—I'd like to reflect briefly on a passage in the Bible that, frankly, has always troubled me. The passage is Matthew 5:48, where Jesus is delivering his Sermon on the Mount and says, "You, therefore, must be perfect, as your heavenly Father is perfect."

"*Perfect*," Jesus says. Exactly how perfect? Perfect like our "heavenly Father," no less! The perfection Jesus asks of us is not a suggestion, not a long-term goal. It is a command: "You, therefore, *must* be perfect!"

Perhaps like you, as a Christian I've struggled for years with Matthew 5:48. For me, it is one of those "hard teachings" that I initially wrestled with and ultimately gave up on. Unreasonable, troublesome, and discouraging, Matthew 5:48 was one of those Bible verses that caused me to feel not connected to, but totally cut off from God. It was a message that made me feel not forgiven, but hopelessly condemned. For me, Matthew 5:48 was the *opposite* of good news. This is, of course, because the command to be perfect was—and is—impossible for me to obey.

Perfect. Such a simple yet spirit-crushing word.

Consider, for example, the trail of human heartache and wreckage caused by striving to meet the impossible standards of "perfection" held up by today's exceedingly image-conscious, achievement-oriented American culture: eating disorders, alcoholism, drug addiction, anxiety, depression, breakdowns, even suicide. What a joyless burden it can be to seek "perfection" in our bodies, our clothing, our work, our homes, our cars, our vacations, our social life, even our volunteer activities. And let's not forget the pressure of keeping up our perfect marriages and perfect children, with their perfect report cards and perfect test scores, who go on to attend perfect colleges and graduate to get perfect jobs, marry perfect spouses, and produce perfect grandchildren!

This tyranny of striving for impossible perfection not only permeates our modern secular culture. As people of faith, who among us hasn't dreamed of and possibly searched for the perfect church, with theologically perfect clergy, who run perfect Bible studies, support perfect missions, and preach a perfect Gospel?

I've been a follower of Jesus for a long time now. But the hard truth is, I'm still more inclined to turn on the television and watch *Dancing with the Stars* than open my Bible. My prayer life is sporadic and dominated by personal concerns. Despite my best intentions, I often forget to pray for others. Good works I do are riddled with self-interest and executed at my convenience, to meet my needs. My initial response to a difficult relationship is more often guilt and anger rather than love and forgiveness. And if it is true that in adversity one discovers one's true self, when confronted with troubles, I find that even after more than thirty years of being a Christian, I am by nature an anxious person who has a hard time trusting God. If anything, I'm like the desperate man in Mark 9:24 who cried out to Jesus, "Lord, I believe. Help my unbelief!"

So what am I to do with Matthew 5:48 and this difficult command from Jesus to be "perfect"?

Imagine my surprise and delight when I recently learned that the Greek word commonly translated as "perfect" in this passage is more accurately translated as "to become *whole*," or "to become *complete*." This means that Jesus asks me not to be perfect, which is humanly impossible, but to be *whole*, which—through His sacrificial, atoning death on the cross—is entirely possible. *Not* because of my flawed and feeble efforts to try to have more faith or do better works, but because of Christ's supreme and absolute act of pure love, I am forgiven and reconciled for all eternity to the Father. *Our* Father. Through the cross, and the cross alone, my broken human heredity is forever altered. Through the cross I am—in a word—made *whole*.

With this new understanding, Matthew 5:48 has gone from being my most troublesome verse of Scripture to one of my favorites—a wellspring of comfort and encouragement for a broken person struggling to make one's way in a fallen world. After all, who doesn't want to be made whole? Who doesn't want to be made complete?

This is very good news, especially as we embark on a New Year. Not to be perfect, but to be *whole* …

Now that's a New Year's resolution I can live with.

Lord, thank You for loving me so much that You called me—in my spiritual brokenness and separation—back into relationship with You through faith in Your Son, Jesus. Thank You for loving me the way I am, totally broken and imperfect, yet—because of Your perfect love through Christ's atoning sacrifice on the Cross—totally whole. As I embark on this new year, help me to grow ever more complete, whole, and healed so I can reach out and touch the hearts of others with Your love.

Holy Smoke! The Amazing Story of How I Quit Smoking

Did you know that in the Bible, there are 139 references to the healing power of God's love? Indeed, when Jesus walked on earth, He brought a two-pronged message of good news. First, He preached the message of *forgiveness*, offering imperfect people reconciliation to God and the promise of eternal life. Second, He *healed* people. Physically, emotionally, relationally, and spiritually, Jesus healed people. On two occasions, He even raised people from the dead!

Forgiveness and healing: two sides of the same coin that, according to the Bible, pretty much sum up what God is all about. Why? Perhaps it is because once we experience God's forgiveness and healing, He can use us to reach out to help others.

I was twenty-four years old, three years out of college, and living and working in Orlando, Florida, when I first experienced God's healing touch …

Driving north on Orlando's South Orange Blossom Trail, I gripped the steering wheel of my lime-green Mustang with my left hand. With my free right hand, I raised the car's cigarette lighter, glowing ruby-red, to the Winston clenched between my lips.

Okay, God, I inhaled the delicious nicotine-laced smoke. *This is my last cigarette. I promise.*

But before I could exhale, I knew it was a promise I would not keep.

I couldn't understand why it was so hard for me to quit smoking. I mean, I really *wanted* to stop. I'd seen the photographs that compared a healthy, pink, nonsmoker's lungs to the blackened lungs of a smoker. I agreed that it was a dirty habit. I worried about my persistent cough and ticklish throat. But no matter how hard I tried to quit, I just wasn't able to do it.

On the car radio, Gordon Lightfoot was crooning on about "The Wreck of the Edmund Fitzgerald." In the rearview mirror, I watched as Tupperware Home Parties World Headquarters—a massive two-story complex with Babylonian-like hanging gardens and an outdoor fountain that looked like a giant dandelion puff—grew smaller and smaller, until it disappeared altogether in a rushing, flat landscape of towering Florida pines.

Turning right into my apartment complex, I passed the swimming pool and clubhouse and pulled into my parking spot. As Todd Rundgren warbled, "Hello, It's Me," I took one last drag on my cigarette and extinguished the butt in the car ashtray. I turned off the radio, grabbed my purse, and bounded up the front steps.

"Hey, *hoo*-ney!" I did my best Ricky Ricardo impression. "I'm *hoo*-me!"

My roommate Sandy and I both worked in the advertising and public relations department at Tupperware, where we traveled around the country interviewing successful women in the business and then wrote up their stories for the company's national magazine, which was read by America's then 250,000 Tupperware ladies.

Prior to joining Tupperware, Sandy had majored in journalism at the University of Florida in Gainesville, and worked as a writer for the *Florida Catholic Reporter*. When she came to work at Tupperware, we hit it off immediately. Both of us loved the Beatles, had big feet (size ten), and—most importantly—we discovered that we shared a simple faith in a loving God. Before we knew it, we became the best of friends. We were so close, in fact, that even though we looked nothing alike (Sandy was brunette and I was blonde), people often asked if we were sisters.

There was only one major difference between us. Sandy did not smoke. And she did not approve of my smoking.

"It's disgusting," she said. "Plus, it'll kill you."

Since becoming a Christian in college, I had flitted from church to church, never staying anywhere long enough to call any one congregation home. I enjoyed visiting churches—not only in and around Orlando but also when traveling on business trips. I liked the way each church had something unique and colorful to offer, like various members in a great big extended family.

At some point during the service of every church I visited, I closed my eyes and silently begged: *Please, God, help me quit smoking.*

I was a Protestant. Sandy was Roman Catholic, a regular churchgoer who frequently invited me to join her for Sunday Mass. On a chilly February morning in 1977, I finally agreed.

Orlando's St. John Vianney Catholic Church was a modest, cement block structure just off the South Orange Blossom Trail. I'd never been inside a Catholic church before. I don't know why, but I had expected something fancier, grand, and gothic—like Chartres, Notre Dame, or Saint Patrick's Cathedral. The service, too, was simple and plain. No Latin. No incense. The sermon, which the priest called a "homily," was about Saint Blaise, a physician who lived in Armenia in the fourth century when Christians were being persecuted by the Romans. Saint Blaise loved Jesus and was martyred for his faith. Because he once saved the life of a young boy who was choking on a fish bone, he became known in the early church as the patron saint for curing sicknesses of the throat.

"Today is February third," said the priest, "the feast day for Saint Blaise. As many of you know, a special blessing of the throat is offered on this day. If any one of you would like to have your throat blessed, please come forward and I will pray for you."

I glanced at Sandy.

She raised her eyebrows as if to ask, *Well?*

I took a deep breath and stepped forward.

What if the priest asks if I'm an official member of his church? I worried. *What if he only blesses Catholics?*

The priest looked at me with compassionate brown eyes. He asked no questions.

"In the name of Jesus," he said, "on this feast day of Saint Blaise, I pray that you no longer suffer from any illness of the throat and that you be healed by God." With his right thumb, he gently marked my forehead with the sign of the cross. "I bless you in the name of the Father, and the Son, and the Holy Spirit."

That was it. I didn't feel much of anything. No heat. No electricity. No spiritual ecstasy. No swooning and falling to the floor. But I was touched by the priest's tenderness and generosity—especially to a visitor.

When I returned to the apartment, I reached into the bottom of my purse and pulled out a half-full pack of cigarettes.

Okay, God. I crumpled up the pack and tossed it into a white wicker wastebasket.

I never smoked again.

Now this is, admittedly, a rather dramatic example of a faith-based healing in the way it was so instantaneous and absolute. Very often healing takes *time*—especially the healing of broken relationships. As with any prayer, sometimes God's answer to a prayer for healing is, "Yes." But sometimes His answer is, "Wait." And still other times it's, "Not now." But no matter what God's answer may be, the *first step* toward healing is to step out in faith, and with the unwavering trust of a child, *ask*.

Is there an area in your life—physical, emotional, relational, or spiritual—that cries out for healing? Talk to God, our great and loving physician, *whose nature it is to heal* and for whom, the Bible says, *nothing is impossible.*

Remember, when it comes to healing, you don't need any special kind or amount of faith. *To believe in God is to believe in healing.*

It's that simple.

Lost and Found

Mom's eyesight was deteriorating, but I didn't know just how bad it had gotten until I saw her stooped in the one-bedroom in-law apartment attached to our house, reaching to pick up something off the floor. She grabbed at it, and then studied her empty thumb and forefinger with a puzzled expression. Again she tried to pinch the glimmering spot on her living-room rug. Nothing. Frowning, she turned to me. Behind the thick lens of her glasses, her blue-green eyes clouded with concern.

"Mom," I said, "it's just a patch of sunlight."

She shook her head, wary to admit something was wrong. That much I could be grateful for. Her attitude was always positive, even determined. She took the challenges of getting old in stride.

"I guess we need to talk," she said.

Back when Mom first moved in with us, I didn't know what it would be like. She was in her late seventies, sophisticated, and fiercely independent, and I was a mom raising two kids in the suburbs. We hadn't lived under the same roof since I left for college. We were unalike in so many ways. She was disorganized and spontaneous. I was a bit of a control freak. My idea of fun as a girl was alphabetizing the books in my bedroom, while she loved to spend a whole afternoon shopping, especially if there was a sale, which I thought was an incredible waste of an afternoon. In junior high, I insisted that my shirt and skirt had to match *exactly*.

"Don't be afraid to mix things up," Mom would say. "Everything doesn't have to match."

Oh yes, it did.

But all that was long ago.

Still, I worried.

Mom liked to entertain friends at the drop of a hat. She loved it when people dropped in unexpectedly for tea and a chat. I liked having company too, but I preferred advance notice—preferably twenty-four hours. Minimum.

At least the apartment adjoining our house had its own kitchen, its own bathroom, and its own front and back doors. It even had its own mini washer/dryer. Thankfully, Mom could still see well enough to drive. With her perky champagne-colored Ford Escort, she would be able to visit friends, shop, and do errands. She would be able to remain independent.

Plus, our kids were thrilled with the idea. The idea of having "Mama B" living right next door, 24/7—her fridge covered with their artwork and photos and filled with sweet treats—was like a dream come true.

Tom and I made sure Mom had her own mailbox and phone, and soon she had her own friends. I could hear their laughter and the sound of the whistling teakettle through the wall. One morning I peeked through her back door window and glimpsed the table she had set for her bridge group, mixing the different patterns of china and glassware. *So like Mom.* For a moment I wished I could be so creative.

Over the years, we found ways to help her deal with her age-related macular degeneration. Tom installed bright halogen lights in her living room. My sister, Laurrie, sent away for a special telephone with big-print numbers. We used colorful plastic adhesive buttons to identify the proper settings on her thermostat, oven, microwave, and washer/dryer. We purchased a high-tech electronic magnifying monitor to help her read her mail. We even found big-print playing cards so Mom could continue playing bridge with her friends.

Mom was able to be independent, and so was I. She could still spend the whole afternoon shopping at a department store sale if she wanted.

Then came that morning I saw her picking a spot of sunlight off the floor.

"Maybe I need more help than I thought," Mom said.

I took a deep breath.

"Yes," I said, "I guess so."

I should have been prepared for this, but I wasn't. I thought things could stay as they were. My mother was going blind, and the doctors said nothing more could be done. I retreated to my kitchen and said a prayer for strength. Then I set out to find a whole new set of resources.

I discovered that our town provided a free service called the "GetAbout" van for seniors who needed transportation. My sister pitched in with frequent visits and trips with Mom to the city. And all those friends whose laughter I heard through the wall … they were only too glad to help. Life took on a sense of new normal. Soon I could hear the teakettle singing on the other side of the wall.

Once, after an afternoon with her friends, Mom came to me, giggling.

"Can you believe it? After our bridge game, the girls had me sit on the floor. They wanted to watch me get up on my own. They couldn't believe I was so limber!"

I could hear the note of pride in her voice. Would I have gotten down on the floor in front of my friends just to prove a point?

"You know," Mom continued, "losing your sight isn't so bad. When you can't see the wrinkles, everyone looks beautiful!"

I looked at her and wondered if I could ever be so accepting of such a scary thing as losing my eyesight. What I once saw as Mom's disorganization now seemed to be an incredible flexibility, a gift for rolling with life's punches, of adapting.

A few weeks before Christmas in 2002, Mom complained of shortness of breath. Her legs hurt, and her usually thin ankles were swollen and stiff. Her blood pressure was high too. The internist sent us to the cardiologist, who sent Mom to get an echocardiogram.

In the examination room, I guided Mom's thin arms through the gaping holes of a huge blue paper gown. How tiny and frail she looked.

When had she gotten so old? I wondered.

Mom had congestive heart failure. Because of her advanced years and high blood pressure, she wasn't a good candidate for heart valve replacement surgery.

*One of the last photos of Mom and me, June 2005,
Grand Central Station, New York City*

"But with proper medication," the cardiologist said to me privately, "she should be able to live another two or three years."

Two or three years, I thought in dismay. *That's so little time!*

One afternoon while sorting a month's supply of Mom's meds into four oversize plastic boxes labeled for the days of the week, my elbow accidentally bumped the top box and sent dozens of pills spilling onto the kitchen floor. Getting down on my hands and knees to retrieve them, I felt overwhelmed with sadness.

God, I prayed, *why does it have to end like this?*

Then, in my heart, I heard a voice stern but tender: *I'm giving you this time with her.*

I listened to the voice with wonder. I repeated the words to myself: *I'm giving you this time with her.*

The whistling teakettle, the noise of the television, the thump of Mom's kitchen cabinet doors came later and later in the day. The friends still visited but not in big groups anymore, and the laughter was quieter. There were no more shopping sprees.

Each morning I peeked through the blinds of Mom's back door and watched her tiny shoulders and chest rise and fall as she slept. How I dreaded the morning that I would find that she wasn't moving. Daily I braced myself for that moment, knowing it had to come. I told myself it would be a blessing if Mom could simply die peacefully in her sleep. Yet I dreaded it. But what was it that I dreaded? Her death? Or that sense of separation—of being so dissimilar—that I was still trying to shake?

She made one last trip to the hospital. At the hospital, a wirelike temporary pacemaker was inserted through a port in my mother's shoulder to regulate her heartbeat—to keep her alive.

But the next day, her organs were failing.

That night, our family gathered around my mother in her hospital bed. Laurrie held one hand. I held the other. Tom stood at the foot of the bed. It wouldn't be long. Katy and Brinck murmured tearful words of love and hugged their grandmother good-bye. She nodded. She was still with us—barely.

I looked down. Her lips moved ever so slightly. I bent my head closer.

"Help me," she whispered.

"We're here, Mom." I squeezed her hand tightly. Her breathing was so slow. I was certain that each breath would be her last. And then ...

"Help me," she said again.

Help you? I looked to my sister and Tom. How could we help her? We'd done everything the doctors said we could. There was nothing more we could do. Then I understood. *My mother wasn't asking for help to live—but to die.* In the strangest way, I felt like a midwife at the bedside of a woman about to give birth—except my mother was laboring to move on to the next life.

"Help me."

Never had I heard two more heartbreakingly beautiful words.

Tears rolled down my cheeks. "We're with you, Mom. I love you. It's all right."

Her breathing grew shallow. Breaths came further apart. I thought of my message from God.

I'm giving you this time with her ...

I remembered how I had feared my mother moving in with us. Instead, it had been an amazing gift. Even now, as her soul was leaving us, I felt something incredible. In the space between those final breaths, that distance I'd always felt between my mother and me evaporated.

For a brief moment, the air in the room seemed to vibrate with the wings of a thousand angels.

And then there was no breath.

She was gone.

That night as we sat around the kitchen table talking and reminiscing, I remembered how I had worried so about my mother's dying. In the end, God, in His great love, had given me the unexpected gift of helping her to be born into her new eternal home in heaven.

Why, I wondered, *had I worried so?* God had known what He was doing all along. His timing and ways were not like mine.

Later that night, as I reached to turn off my bedside lamp, I thought again about how different I'd felt from my mother when I was young. But now something unexpected and spontaneous crept into my mind. Tomorrow I would go to one of the sales that Mom so loved at her favorite store, and I would shop for just the right dress to wear for her funeral …

All afternoon if necessary.

The Black Dress

"Time of death?"

The funeral director held his pen in the air, his eyebrows arched expectantly.

Such a simple question.

But no one answered.

"I've got it here somewhere." I fumbled in my bag for the hospital form the doctor on duty had given me the night before.

Tom, Laurrie, and I were seated around a coffee table in the front parlor of New Canaan's Hoyt F. Funeral Home. The atmosphere was hushed and subdued. It was a sunny August afternoon, but the room was lit in a way that you couldn't tell whether it was day or night outside. My mother's body was in the next room. It had been her wish that her remains be interred alongside my father's in the columbarium at Arlington National Cemetery in Virginia. We had come to the funeral home for one last good-bye.

"I can call the hospital if you can't remember the time of death," the director said. "But I need it for the death certificate."

"No, no, I'm sure I've got it here somewhere."

I thought back to the night before in the hospital room, when my mother had died. But the *exact* time of death? Who could say? Yes, there had been a last breath. A final heartbeat. But after that? Her life had simply slipped away like water through a crack in time, finding its way to infinity's timeless ocean. It had all been so mysterious. Was it her soul that had left her body? Or her body that had left her soul? I remembered the sense of angels being in the room with us and shivered.

The veil between heaven and earth had been so thin as to be transparent. One thing I knew for certain: My mother had *not* died when the doctor, wearing a stethoscope around his neck and carrying a clipboard in his hand, had gently ushered us out of the room and closed the curtains around her bed. By then she had long departed this world. By then she not only had arrived in heaven—she had been there forever.

I pulled a flimsy yellow document out of my handbag, put on my reading glasses, and ran my finger down the lines of information.

```
Name: Elizabeth Johnson Brinckerhoff
Date of Birth: June 20, 1915
Place of Birth: Niagara Falls, New York
Cause of Death: Heart Failure
```

"Time of Death: Ten thirty-five p.m.," I read.

"Thank you." The funeral director scribbled down the information, clicked his pen, and stood up. "Would you like to view the body now?"

No! I thought. *Everything is happening too fast.* But I nodded and followed Laurrie and Tom into the viewing room.

Wrapped in a white sheet, my mother's body was lying on a flat slab—lifeless and uninhabited, like a dress that she had suddenly stepped out of and left lying in a rumpled pile. *Like the grave clothes in the tomb*, I thought.

Yes, her body was there. But the person who had been my mother was gone—irretrievably, absolutely gone. The sense of separation and loss was so acute as to be almost unbearable.

"Oh, Mommy, Mommy, Mommy," I cried. The words came from some deep, forgotten place in my soul. I couldn't remember ever having called my mother "Mommy." But suddenly I was so very young … six … four … two years old. Such a very little girl—utterly brokenhearted and lost without my mother.

I stroked her auburn curls and gently pulled at them to frame her face, just the way she liked—one last time.

"Good-bye," I whispered, kissing her cheek.

And then it was time to go.

Back home, my sister and I entered the apartment where our mother had spent the last twelve years of her life. We were exhausted but determined to pick up the place and prepare it for our out-of-town relatives, who would be arriving later in the week for the funeral service.

By the time Laurrie pulled out of the driveway to return to her apartment in the city, the summer sun hung low, a glowing crimson ball in a golden sky. I looked at the clock on the kitchen wall: *Eight o'clock!* I remembered the promise I'd made to myself the night before to find a dress for my mother's funeral. If I wanted to make the sale at Lord & Taylor, I was going to have to hurry.

As I rode the escalator up to the department store's second floor, I said a little prayer. *Please, God, help me find the right dress.*

But after searching the racks of dresses, I came up with nothing.

Just my luck, I thought. Everything was either the wrong size, or too short, or too dressy, or too expensive. My heart sank with discouragement.

I was about to leave when I took one last look at the clearance rack. And there, among a jumble of picked-over garments, was the perfect dress—black with a delicate lace bodice and cap sleeves. A bright orange sticker on the tag indicated that the dress had been marked down three times from its original steep price. But would it fit?

"Do you need any help?" The saleswoman looked at her watch. "I don't mean to rush you, but we'll be closing soon."

"I'll just be a minute," I said, heading for the dressing room.

Amazingly, the dress fit perfectly.

At the checkout counter, I handed the saleswoman the dress.

"How pretty," she said, punching the buttons on the register. "And it's a bargain, too. Seventy-five percent off from the last marked down price."

"Great!" I said. "Oh, wait. I've got a coupon." I fished in my purse for a fifteen percent-off coupon that my mother had given me just days earlier.

The saleswoman scanned the coupon, punched a few more buttons, and looked at the screen with wide eyes.

"Oh my," she said, and handed me the sales receipt.

I stared in disbelief at the amount: $7.99.

"If only my mother could see this," I said. "She always loved a good bargain. The dress is for her—funeral ..."

And then I fell apart.

Katy, all grown up

The Butterfly's Secret

One day I received a phone call from the editor-in-chief at Guideposts Books. She had read a story about my mom and me that I had written for *Guideposts* and asked if I might consider expanding it into a full-length book. "A memoir," is what she called it.

Me? Write a memoir?

For a fleeting moment, my heart fluttered with excitement at the idea. And then, just as quickly, I was terrified.

It was one thing to write a magazine-length story about my mom and me. But to fully explore the complicated terrain of our relationship would mean having to be scrupulously honest—sometimes painfully so. It would mean publicly acknowledging that there were many aspects of my life that weren't so perfect. It would mean revealing that my beloved father suffered and died a tragic, too-early death from alcoholism—not to mention my own battle with a stubborn eating disorder and lifetime struggle with worry and anxiety. It would mean admitting that during the later years of my mother's life, it wasn't always easy being squeezed in the middle of the "sandwich generation," pressed on both sides to meet the needs of my aging mom while also caring for my two children and husband.

Yes, I agreed with the editor, the purpose of the book would be to encourage others struggling with similar issues. And yes, I understood that the overarching message of the book would be about the amazing healing and redemptive power of God's love. How in God's economy, nothing in life goes to waste. How *everything* in life has value—even the pain—and how something beautiful and good can come from life's most difficult circumstances and mistakes. And yes, after three decades of writing hundreds of inspirational stories for *Guideposts*—albeit mostly *other people's* stories—I understood the incredible power of the first-person narrative to reach out and touch the human heart. Still, because of the very personal nature of the project—okay, let's face it, because of the potentially embarrassing self-disclosures that the book would require—I wasn't so sure.

"I need some time to think about it," I said.

Dear God, I prayed, as I hung up the phone. *Show me what You want me to do.*

A few days later, I was walking with my daughter Katy in a local park. At the center of the park was an old estate with a formal flower garden in full bloom, lush with sunshiny yellow dahlias, blue hydrangeas, pink roses ... and everywhere butterflies, fluttering from one magnificent blossom to another.

Katy and I became transfixed by a beautiful aquamarine butterfly that didn't seem at all to mind our presence. Fascinated, we leaned closer and observed as the butterfly delicately lit on the edge of a creamy pink petal and extended her long, needlelike, thread-thin proboscis to sip sweet nectar from the blossom's center. It was like watching a Discovery Channel nature program. We could even see the microscopic fuzz on her jet-black antennae and the trembling of her translucent jewel-tone gossamer wings, like a matched pair of two miniature stained-glass windows.

For several seconds we fell silent, caught up in the wonder of the moment.

"Isn't it amazing," Katy whispered, "how she so naturally and effortlessly does what she was created to do?"

"Yes." I nodded. My daughter is a quiet soul—the phrase "still waters run deep" comes to mind—and when she speaks, she has a way of coming up with the most surprisingly and delightfully profound observations.

"I wonder ..." Katy mused as we closed the garden gate behind us and headed toward home, "if God can create a butterfly so perfectly for His purposes, what do you think He's created us to do?"

That night, as I reached to turn off my bedside lamp and closed my eyes, all I could think about was the beautiful butterfly and my daughter's provocative question.

How can we know what God has created us to do? How can we discern His will for our lives—day in and day out, in ways large and small?

I remembered a friend telling me once that God has actually provided us with a natural indicator for discerning his purposes, and that is *enthusiasm*—a word that literally means "to be inspired and indwelled by God." That's why, my friend explained, when you experience enthusiasm, it's a good idea to *pay attention*. That fluttering sensation in your heart is God's spirit dancing. It's God's way of saying, *"Yes! Go for it!"*

I thought of the memoir I'd been asked to write and remembered how initially my heart fluttered—*like a thousand butterflies!*—at the idea. For years I had been writing other people's stories. Maybe God was trying to tell me that now it was time to write my own.

Okay, God, I prayed before drifting off to sleep. *I'll do it. Thank You for this life You've given me. Now I'm just going to give it back to You as honestly as I can for You to do what You want with it.*

Now that the book, *Lost & Found: One Daughter's Story of Amazing Grace*, has been published, I believe it was worth the effort. Just the other day a woman wrote the most beautiful letter, saying that my story had helped her make the decision to have her aging mother move in with her. She said that she had been wrestling with the issue for months and that reading *Lost & Found* was like getting a sign from God about what she should do.

Are you trying to figure out what God has created you to do?

Ask yourself this simple question: *What is it that excites you and fills your heart with enthusiasm?*

Perhaps it's volunteering to work at your local soup kitchen ... Or gathering friends together for a spur-of-the-moment potluck supper ... Or teaching Sunday school ... Or taking a day off from work to share time with a loved one ... Or baking cookies for your neighbor who's sick ... Or sending a cheerful note to a discouraged friend ... Or signing up for yoga classes ... Or adopting a cat or dog from the animal shelter ... Or running for local public office ... Or leading a Bible study ... Or joining a reading group ... Or taking a course at your local community college ... Or setting aside time each day to work on that book you always wanted to write ...

Whatever it is, just follow your natural-born enthusiasm—God's gift of His guiding Spirit, abiding like a thousand butterflies in your heart. I promise it will be His greatest joy and delight to show you the way.

Squeezed in the Middle: How to Care for an Aging Parent in the Sandwich Generation

Did you know that nearly half of today's 77 million baby boomers have one or more aging parent *and* children under the age of twenty-one living at home? And this is a number that experts say is rapidly increasing.

I know that when my widowed mother first moved into the in-law apartment attached to our house, I wasn't so sure it was going to work out. This is because for as long as I could remember, "prickly" was the best word to describe our relationship. When I was a little girl, I remember thinking how my mother and I were like two negatively polarized magnets—like the little plastic apple and orange stuck on our refrigerator door—fighting against an invisible force that worked to push us apart.

I loved my mother, but we were different in so many ways.

What, I wondered, *would it be like with Mom living so close, with nothing separating us but a thin wall?*

When it comes to caring for an aging parent, I am no expert. Perhaps like some of you, I'm just an everyday daughter with my own story to share. So, looking back, here are the six most valuable lessons I learned and that I hope might serve as a source of hope and encouragement for you too.

Living so close-by, Mom became an important part of our children's lives

One: Flexibility is key ... Expect the unexpected.

There were many times when caring for my mother reminded me of when I was a new parent, in that I often found myself paddling in uncharted waters, "making it up" as I went along. Just as there is no one-size-fits-all manual for new parents because every child is different, there is no one-size-fits-all manual for caring for an aging parent. Consider the infinite number of variables at work in each situation ...

For starters, there is the nature of the adult child-parent relationship. Is it close? Or distant? Healthy? Or unhealthy? Other factors to consider are: the adult child and parent's financial circumstances; the adult child and parent's housing situation; the adult child and parent's mental, emotional, physical, and spiritual health; as well as the availability and willingness or unwillingness of the adult child's *siblings* to also pitch in and help care for the aging parent. Complicating matters even more is the fact that all of these unique variables are maddeningly fluid and ever-changing!

Inevitably, just when I thought I had everything figured out and had established a smooth-as-glass daily routine for my mother and me, a new (often health-related) challenge would crop up, shattering our presumptions and challenging our boundaries. When this happened, we would have to pick up the pieces and start over, working together to create what we came to call a "new normal."

For example, when my mother came to live with us at age seventy-eight, her vision was poor due to age-related macular degeneration, but she was still able to drive. Because she could drive, she was able to maintain her independence—and so was I.

But the day inevitably came when Mom came to me and said, "I don't think I should be driving anymore."

With that one simple sentence—"I don't think I should be driving anymore"—the familiar day-to-day routine and healthy boundaries we had worked so hard to build suddenly became as blurred as my mother's vision, and for a moment I felt as though I couldn't breathe.

If Mom couldn't drive, who was going to take her to the grocery store? To doctors' appointments? To the hair salon? To the dry cleaners? To visit her friends?

My mother was going to *need help*. Lots of it. My life was already so busy with two teenagers, work, a new puppy, and managing my own household. *How was I ever going to meet my mother's needs?*

Two: Don't be afraid or ashamed to ask for help.

For a while, I tried to do it all myself. But inevitably feelings of burden, resentment, and *guilt* (guilt for feeling burdened and resentful!) piled up like dirty laundry. It didn't help when some well-meaning friend would inevitably say, "Oh Kitty, you're such a *good* daughter to be taking such good care of your mother." *No, I'm not,* I wanted to say. *Goodness has nothing to do with it.* If I were honest, I would have to admit that much of what I did for my mother was more about daughterly duty than daughterly love. And there were days when I felt absolutely trapped.

Being a person of faith, I picked up my Bible to look for guidance, which initially left me feeling only more confused and racked with guilt—especially when I came across that particularly onerous Fifth Commandment: "Honor your father and mother."

"What exactly does that mean?" I groused to my husband. "To *honor* your mother? I mean, what exactly does God want from me? Is there such a thing as giving up too much of one's life for another? Sometimes I feel like there's just not enough of me to go around."

"I don't know," said Tom. "Maybe you should talk to someone. You're not the only person dealing with an aging parent. Maybe there's someone who can help you."

Three: Know you are not alone.

The next day, I made an appointment to visit with my minister, the Reverend Gail Carlsen. She was an expert in geriatric pastoral concerns, beloved by many older members of the congregation for her open door and listening ear. Now she leaned forward and listened intently as I told her about feeling overwhelmed about meeting my mother's ever-increasing needs.

"Oh, Kitty," she said. "It's so good you came to talk. You're a classic example of a woman trapped in the sandwich generation."

Well, I'd heard of the lost generation. The greatest generation. The Pepsi generation. The me generation. Generation X. But the *sandwich* generation?

"What's that?" I asked.

"You're being squeezed by responsibilities on both generational ends," Gail explained. "You're caught between being a wife and mother and taking care of your own mother. I imagine sometimes you must feel pretty squished." She smiled sympathetically.

"Yes!" I agreed. "There are days when that's exactly how I feel."

"You ask about the Fifth Commandment and what it means to honor your mother," she said. "It's a good question.

"The word honor means *to respect, to hold in high esteem*. It can also imply a certain formality—even distance. God understands that you have primary responsibilities to your husband and children. He understands that you can't be all things to all people all the time—and I don't think He expects you to be."

She walked over to a tall file cabinet, opened the top drawer, and pulled out a thick manila folder.

"It's important to realize that *you're not alone*," she said. "As people live longer, more and more of us find ourselves caring for aging parents.

"The *good news* is that there are many resources available to help your mom—*and you*." She wrapped her arm around me. "You know, the reason God put us here on earth is to help each other."

With Gail's help, I learned that our town provided a free service for seniors who needed transportation, called the "GetAbout Van." She also introduced me to our town's senior outreach worker, a wonderful woman named Melba Neville, who was not only a registered nurse but also an expert on how to access local, county, state, and government assistance for every age-related issue imaginable.

Three mornings a week, we employed the reasonably-priced services of a wonderful company called Home Instead, who dispatched a cheerful, energetic woman named Debbie to help my mother with her correspondence, sorting photos, odd jobs, and errands.

My sister, Laurrie, pitched in with frequent visits and took my mother shopping and to her appointments in the city with a doctor who practiced "integrated medicine" and gave her special vitamins for her eyes. And all those ladies who liked to stop by for tea and a chat—my mother's many friends—they were only too glad to help too.

Although my mother could no longer drive, once again our life together took on a sense of "new normal."

Four: Look for hidden blessings.

Just the other day, I overheard our now-adult daughter, Katy, describe the years that my mother lived in the in-law apartment attached to our house as "three generations of women living together." I had never thought of it that way before!

Our daughter, Katy, and our son, Brinck, were my mother's only grandchildren, and she loved them very much. Because she lived so close by, she was a constant presence in their lives. When they were young, her back door was always open for their spontaneous visits, and she kept her fridge covered with their artwork and photos and filled with sweet treats. As the children grew older, she became their elder, trusted confidante.

She was a nonjudgmental "parental option" for them—always willing to listen and not shy about dispensing her opinions, advice, and hard-earned wisdom. Sometimes I had to laugh. My daughter has a natural fashion sense, which she certainly did not get from me! But she was able to share this with her *very stylish* grandmother.

As years passed, our children were exposed to the challenges and heartaches associated with growing old, and—following their grandmother's death—the acute grief experienced with the loss of a loved one. The good news is that our children were also able to witness firsthand a woman who faced growing old with incredible grace and optimism. In this intergenerational sense, my mother was a wonderful role model—not only for her grandchildren but for us all.

Five: Remember God's promise … All things work together for good.

I read somewhere once that courage is not about being fearless but about taking action and moving forward despite being afraid. My mother, in the positive way she dealt with her blindness, is probably the most courageous person I have ever known. And here's the thing: Had I not been given the opportunity to observe her closely, day in and day out, as she confronted the challenges and losses associated with aging—especially blindness—I never would have fully appreciated her strength, optimism, and courage. I only hope when I am older that I can be so brave.

When my mother moved into the in-law apartment attached to our house, I initially wasn't so sure it was a good idea. As it turned out, having my mother live next door to us for the last twelve years of her life was a surprising, beautiful, and totally unexpected *gift*.

Despite our differences, by the time my mother passed away at age ninety, I had grown to respect, appreciate, understand, and love her to a degree that I would never have dreamed possible. Today, looking back, I can see how God was walking alongside the two of us all along, working in the situation for His good and loving purposes.

Six: Good news! It's never too late to begin again.

Are you an adult child who suffers from stress in your relationship with your aging parent? If so, try to not feel unduly guilty or ashamed. Parent-child conflict and stress is very common—it's part of being human.

It helps to remember that God, who loves and cares for *you*, also loves and cares for your aging parent, and He is eager to work in *both your hearts* for healing ... forgiveness ... understanding ... compassion ... patience ... reconciliation ...whatever it is that you need.

The good news is that it is never too late to begin a new and positive chapter in your relationship.

Mom and Katy, New York City

Katy, Brinck and Mom ... enjoying a "Sandwich Generation" togetherness moment!

Counting My Blessings on Mother's Day

I read somewhere recently that the loudest voice a child will ever hear belongs to his or her mother.

I know when I was growing up, my mother had lots of advice and opinions—certain sayings she repeated so frequently that over the years I came to think of them as "Mom's Maxims." In no particular order, they went something like this:

- *"Don't be a snoop."* (Most often intoned around Christmas and birthdays.)
- *"Remember, you represent the Brinckerhoff family."* ('Nuff said!)
- *"Only a fool tells* all *he knows."* (And no one wants to be a fool!)
- *"Know when to leave a party."* (This one was intended more for grown-ups.)

But there was one of Mom's Maxims that stood apart from all the others, because it wasn't just words. It was something I watched her put into action, day in and day out: *"When you're feeling blue, count your blessings and do something nice for someone else."*

The first time I heard my mother say this, I remember hoping that it didn't mean that every time she did something nice for someone else (which was quite often) it was because she was feeling blue!

My beautiful mother, Elizabeth Johnson Brinckerhoff

To this day, when I think of my mother, the first image that comes to mind is of her standing in the kitchen wearing her favorite blue gingham apron, her red hair dusty with flour, wrapping cellophane over a pretty paper plate of fresh-baked cookies or chocolate cake, to take to a friend who was "down in the dumps" … or dealing with an illness … or grieving the loss of a loved one. The effect of my mother's brief visits—she stayed only long enough to drop off her gift of comfort food and offer a hug—was to let her friends know, quite simply, that they were appreciated … cared for … loved.

When the day came that failing vision caused my mother to no longer be able to drive, she gave me the honor of assisting her with her deliveries. And when the day came that she no longer had the strength to bake, she still found time to write encouraging notes and leave cheerful phone messages for her many friends.

My mother did these things right up until the day she died.

Looking back, I believe that it was simply her nature to reach out to others with kindness. It was instinctive. As it says in the Bible, her "left hand didn't know what the right hand was doing" when she baked those cookies, arranged them on a pretty plate, and delivered them to her friends. (See Matthew 6:2–4.) It was, in the end, an extraordinarily beautiful and unselfconscious demonstration of *putting love into action*. And it was, by far, the most important thing my mother ever taught me.

So on this Mother's Day, when I find myself feeling a bit blue because Mom isn't here, I'm going to take her advice and count my blessings—which start, of course, with being grateful to God for giving me the gift of such a good mother!

And what about "doing something nice for someone else"?

I hope that sharing this story with you has helped to do just that.

Max and the Lost Keys

Let me begin by introducing you to our dog Mighty Maximus Slattery—better known as Max.

Max is not like most dogs. Pointers, for example, point. Retrievers retrieve. Hounds hunt. These highly talented and useful breeds behave this way because they are all, as my husband, Tom, likes to say, *real* dogs. No, if anything, our dog is more like a—a—oh dear, I'm afraid words fail me. Our children say Max is like an ewok.

Max is a pug. A roly-poly, fawn-colored pug. He is a pug, like most pugs, that primarily excels at sleeping, eating, and making us laugh. When we first brought Max home as a ten-week-old ball of fluff, we knew from the dog book that pugs were classified as having "fair intelligence" and being only "moderately trainable"—as opposed to border collies, poodles, German shepherds, Labradors, and golden retrievers, which are, as everyone knows, dog geniuses. But over time, we were delighted to discover that Max would do practically *anything* for a treat, and he quickly acquired a repertoire of tricks, including, "Roll over," "Spin around," "Bow," and "Dancey-dancey." Did I mention there's something about Max that inspires baby talk?

Max has other talents too. We call them his "special abilities," like the X-Men superheroes. For some inexplicable (and delicious) reason, Max smells like Fritos corn chips. He also possesses the uncanny power, at will, to utterly *undo* us—like Antonio Banderas's "Puss in Boots" character in the *Shrek* cartoons—when he cocks his head and makes his bottomless black eyes go all big and sad. Apparently Max was born with an overabundance of something zoologists actually call the "cute factor." With his large, round head, flat face, floppy ears, and big, front-facing eyes, Max ranks right up there in animal kingdom cuteness with pandas, koala bears, and baby seals.

So other than being irresistibly cute, what good is a pug?

It was the seventeenth-century Dutch who, along with their boatloads of exotic teas and spices, delivered the first pugs to northern Europe from China, where they were originally bred as mini-mastiffs for the amusement of the emperor. Today it is generally agreed that pugs are the clowns of the dog world. With his wrinkled brow and soulful eyes, Max does bear a rather startling likeness to the late king of clowns, Emmett Kelley Jr. A few years ago, a friend sent me a card with a ridiculous photo of a pug dressed up like Yoda from *Star Wars* that said, "Pugs are living proof that God has a sense of humor."

Keep that thought in mind as I tell you my story ...

It hadn't been a good week.

A freakish tropical storm where we live in Connecticut had caused the gutters on our old house to overflow, which in turn caused a flood in our basement, including the carpeted rec room, which now smelled like wet socks.

I was also anxiously awaiting—okay, worrying obsessively about—test results for a recent CT scan of Tom's lungs. A month earlier, he had briefly been hospitalized with what was originally diagnosed as pneumonia. Now the doctor said he wasn't sure. Maybe it was something else. Something serious.

And then I lost my keys. Well, I didn't actually "lose" my keys. To say that one has "lost" one's keys usually means that one has merely "misplaced" one's keys. Over the years, I suspect that I've misplaced—and eventually found—my keys hundreds of times.

No, my keys *vanished*. One minute they were on the kitchen table next to my grocery list, securely attached to a brown braided-leather key chain. And when I looked again, after saying good-bye to the gutter cleaners and the carpet cleaners—a veritable swarm of workers who had all arrived at the same time ... *Poof!* The keys were gone. It was as though their resting spot on the kitchen table was some sort of invisible portal to another dimension that had suddenly opened up and sucked them far, far away.

For the next two hours, I turned the house upside down and inside out looking for my keys. First, I got down on my hands and knees and scanned the kitchen floor. Nothing. Then I dumped and scrutinized the contents of my purse. Twice. Yes, I checked my pockets. And yes, I checked the car. And although I knew it made no sense, I also checked the refrigerator, freezer, pantry, and oven.

I called my friend Sara, told her what had happened, and asked her if she would please say a little prayer—for the missing keys and for Tom's test results—which she did, right there over the phone. Praying helped me feel a bit less anxious about Tom, but did nothing for my state of mind about the keys.

As I hung up the phone, I was seized by an unpleasant thought: *What if one of the workers took the keys?*

Frantic, I phoned Tom at work and in a rush of words told him what had happened.

"You'd better call a locksmith," he said calmly.

So I did. At least now we didn't have to worry about being robbed.

Days passed. Still, I couldn't stop wondering about the missing keys. In my mind's eye, I could picture the brown braided-leather key chain so clearly—feel its supple softness, worn smooth as a pebble after years of being tumbled around my purse. The keys were the first thing I thought of in the morning, and the last thing I thought of before going to sleep. Where could they have gone?

A week later on a Saturday afternoon, Tom was standing in the kitchen doorway with dog leash in hand.

"Can you believe the way those keys never turned up?" I asked him.

"Good thing we had the locks changed," he replied. "Max and I are going for a walk. Wanna come?"

"Sure."

We live on a busy street with lots of traffic, and when Max goes for a walk, he wears a leash attached to his red harness. Max wears a harness because his head and neck are the same size—I guess you could say he doesn't have a neck—and a regular dog collar too easily slips off. Because of his flat nose and thick fur, in warmer weather Max sometimes gets overheated and we have to *carry* him home, which gives a whole new meaning to the phrase "taking the dog for a walk."

Anyhow, on this particular afternoon, Max assumed his usual pokey pace, meandering along the sidewalk, stopping to sniff (endlessly) every tree trunk, utility pole, and fire hydrant along the way. We strolled past our neighbors' homes and then crossed the street, where an empty house was undergoing a renovation. The yard was overgrown and unkempt, littered with lumber and bricks.

Abruptly, Max veered off the sidewalk and onto the overgrown lot, tugging fiercely on his leash.

"No-no, Max," I said. "Stay on the sidewalk."

He regarded me imploringly with his Antonio Banderas eyes and pulled harder, suddenly lurching forward onto the lawn and flopping down on his belly with his legs splayed out. Panting, he closed his eyes and luxuriated in the cool softness of the tall grass and weeds.

"*C'mon*, Max," I pleaded, pulling his leash.

Stubbornly he resisted and became twenty unmovable pounds of dead weight as he pressed his black velvet chin even more firmly into the ground.

"I don't know what's gotten into him," said Tom. "I guess we'd better pick him up and go home."

As I bent down to pick Max up, I glimpsed something buried deep in the weeds next to Max's head—something that looked very much like a bit of brown braided-leather.

No, I thought. *This can't be possible.*

I tugged gently—as though pulling a small carrot out of the ground—and there they were, covered with dirt. My keys.

"*Oh, my gosh!*" I yelped. "*I can't believe it!*"

I screamed so loudly that pedestrians across the street looked over with alarm. "No problem!" I called to them, grinning ecstatically, dangling the keys in the air. "Our dog found my keys!" They must have thought I was crazy. And for a moment, I wondered if I was. *How in the world did Max—a dog who barely has a nose, let alone a sense of smell—manage to lead us precisely to this tiny patch of weeds and grass?*

Max and the Lost Keys

Mighty Max with the lost keys!

"Good dog!" I picked Max up and buried my face in his soft fur.

He waggled his cinnamon-bun tail and snorted happily.

As the three of us turned and headed toward home, Tom speculated that perhaps the keys had, indeed, been taken by one of the workers.

"It would have been nice," Tom smiled wryly, "if Max could have found the keys *before* we changed the locks."

Later that afternoon, the phone rang. It was the doctor with good news. The CT scan had revealed that Tom was healing nicely after all. Not to worry, the doctor said. Tom would be fine.

That night as I lay in bed, I thought back over the week and remembered my prayer over the telephone with my friend Sara.

Oh, Kitty, I heard God's whisper. *When will you learn to stop worrying and trust Me? You know I always hear you when you pray. And you know I always answer. In My own time. In my own way. Sometimes it is in the most unlikely and surprising ways ...*

Sometimes even with a pug.

Learning to Let Go in a "Tiger Mom" World

It is every parent's fantasy—especially in today's hyper achievement-oriented "Tiger Mom" world—that his or her child will move joyfully and effortlessly through life, leaping from success to success, from one mountaintop experience to the next.

As parents, it is tempting to believe that if we simply take intentional steps to improve on the parenting we received, our children will be protected from life's hurts and troubles—at least the kind of hurts and troubles we may have experienced as children. There is a certain irresistible logic to this idea. Because we love our children, we want to believe we somehow possess the power—through our parenting—to guarantee their happiness, wellness, and success in life.

For example, the parent who grew up in a household where there was the stress of chronic debt and arguments about money will try to make sure his or her financial house is in order. The parent who grew up in a household where education was not valued will want to make sure that his or her children study hard and do well in school. The parent who grew up in a household that was shattered by infidelity or divorce will do everything she or he can to create a sense of stability and security.

In my case, because I lost my beloved father to the terrible disease of alcoholism, I made sure that ours was a household where there was no parental substance abuse. Because I grew up in a household where problems were sometimes denied, I worked hard to encourage open and transparent communication in our family. Because I grew up in a household where faith was not so important, I made a conscious effort to introduce our two children to God at an early age and nurtured that faith throughout their growing-up years.

These were all well-intentioned efforts. But the older I get—or perhaps I should say the older our *children* get—the more humbled I am to discover that no matter how many steps my husband and I might take to ensure our children's smooth-going in life, they must ultimately find their own way. Despite all that we might do with the hope of inoculating them from life's pain and troubles, they will still have their own hurtful experiences. They will still make mistakes. This is because our children—like us—are human.

Because our children are human, we can be sure they will struggle with illnesses and accidents. They may become entangled in negative relationships. They may make poor choices, sometimes with serious and lasting consequences. They may even choose to reject God.

When these things happen, our children will give us sleepless nights. They will anger and disappoint us. Sometimes they will break our hearts. Make no mistake: Being a parent is not for the faint of heart. But I am beginning to learn that it is in the pain of trying times that our children are also learning critical life lessons and that their character is being forged.

As a person of faith, I am learning to trust that even in the midst of the most difficult circumstances, God is working in our children's lives. I am learning to internalize Paul's message of hope to the early believers in Rome when he wrote, "All [not some, but *all!*] things work together for good for those who love the Lord and are called according to His purpose" (Romans 8:28).

Just the other day, I was talking about these things to a good friend (and mother of four grown sons) when she suddenly turned to me and said, "Oh, Kitty. You worry way too much. Let me let you in on a little secret. Our kids really don't belong to us. Our kids belong to God. He's their true Father, and He gave them to us on loan for a season."

My friend went on to say that despite all our human flaws, God trusts us to do the best parenting we can until the moment comes—and it may very well be a dark and desperate moment—when all we can do is release our children in faith, with prayer, back to their Father, who loves them more deeply and more perfectly than we ever can.

My friend is right. Letting go is so much easier when I remember that I am releasing my children to a deeply personal God who has every hair on their head counted. A loving Father who sends His angels to watch over them and who has every day of their lives written in His Book of Life. Most importantly, I am surrendering my children to a God who knows far better than I what's best for them. As the prophet Isaiah wrote thousands of years ago, "'For my thoughts are not your thoughts, neither are your ways my ways,' says the Lord. 'For as the heavens are higher than the earth, so are my ways higher than your ways and my thoughts higher than your thoughts'" (Isaiah 55:8–9).

To recognize that I don't always know what's best for my adult children but trust that their loving Father in heaven does … This, I am beginning to learn, is the secret of letting go.

Prayer for Adult Children

Thank You, Father, for how You love my adult children
far more deeply and perfectly than I ever can.
Help me remember that they don't belong to me. They belong to You.
You entrusted them to me on loan,
and I—in my brokenness and human failing—have done the best I can.
Help me now to give my children back to You.
Help me also to understand that now is the time for my role as
a human parent to recede,
while Your role as my children's perfect parent increases.
When I start to get worried, anxious, and controlling, help me
to let go and get out of Your way.
Help me to stand back and watch in faith, awe, and total trust
as You work Your perfect will in my adult children's lives.

The Sixpence

Something old

Something new

Something borrowed

Something blue…

And a silver sixpence in her shoe.

—Author Unknown

Katy and Matthew

Photo credit: Michele Shirley

Engaged! Our daughter, Katy, was engaged!

My initial reaction was an irrepressible bubbling up of so many happy emotions, like a freshly uncorked bottle of champagne ... *Joy! Excitement! Anticipation!*

But my happiness fizzled when I shared the news with a well-meaning friend who said, "Oh, Kitty, congratulations! You're going to be a wonderful mother of the bride!"

Mother of the bride?

I'd heard of "father of the bride." But mother of the bride? For some reason, the phrase filled me with anxiety—and a wistful sadness.

What did I know about being a mother of the bride?

I remembered my big sister's wedding back when I was in high school and how my mother knew all the traditions and was the consummate mother of the bride. "We'll need 'something old, something new, something borrowed, something blue,'" she recited the age-old poem, including the last line, "'and a silver sixpence in her shoe.'" She helped my sister pick out invitations, her gown, the bridesmaid dresses, the photographer, and flowers—everything. Mom even found an authentic English sixpence for my sister to tuck in her shoe.

Several years later, when I got engaged to Tom in Minnesota, it was a different story. As Charles Dickens might say, it was "the best of times and the worst of times" for our family. It was the best of times because Tom was a wonderful man. It was the worst of times because my beloved father was terminally ill. Because of Dad's illness, Tom and I decided to forgo a traditional wedding. My parents were in Florida, but Dad was too sick to come to the ceremony even if we'd had it there, and I knew Mom didn't want to leave his side. So Tom and I decided to get married as simply as possible in Minnesota.

We didn't have to come up with a guest list or send out invitations. There were no bridesmaids, no white dress with a veil, and no silver sixpence in my open-toed shoes. Tom's big brother gave me away. We didn't have a big reception, and our honeymoon was one night at the Stillwater Inn, with free fireworks thrown in because it happened to be the Fourth of July.

Tom and me on our wedding day, July 4, 1980

We were married just over a week when my mother telephoned with the sad news that Dad had died. Even so, in the midst of her heartache and loss, she had taken the time to send out engraved wedding announcements to family and friends.

"Oh, Mom," I said to her after the funeral, "I can't believe you went to all that effort, especially after all you've been through. It's too much."

But that was Mom. "Don't be silly," she replied. "It was the right thing to do. Plus, it made me happy." She smiled. "You know how much I love weddings." Her eyes misted up as she reached for my hand and squeezed it tightly. "I only wish I could have been at yours."

How she would have celebrated her only granddaughter's wedding! I thought.

But now Mom was gone, too. She had spent her last years living in the in-law apartment attached to our house, and she and Katy had been close. "Mama B!" Katy always called her, dropping in to visit. Now all I could think of was how much Mom would have enjoyed helping Katy with her wedding preparations and seeing her walk down the aisle.

With each passing day, my worries about being an adequate mother of the bride mounted. The more I learned from friends and books and wedding websites, the more overwhelmed I felt. What did I know about invitations, flowers, photographers, music, and menus? If only Mom were still here, she would have known what to do.

Lord, I said, *You're going to have to help me.*

One afternoon, while rummaging in the bottom drawer of my jewelry box for a lost earring, my fingers touched something soft and silky—a tiny zippered coin purse. It had belonged to my mother. I hadn't seen it in years.

How had it gotten in my jewelry box? I wondered.

I examined the purse closely. With its delicate Asian-patterned fabric and tiny silver zipper, the purse was perfect for Katy. She would love it. Her birthday was just around the corner. I would set it aside and give it to her then.

I was about to put the purse back in my jewelry box when I felt a small bump in the fabric. Curious, I gently tugged at the tiny zipper, which slid open with ease. To my surprise, tucked inside the purse was a carefully folded piece of paper, yellow with age. A note.

Hands trembling, slowly, carefully, I unfolded it. It was on Mom's stationery, with her name engraved at the top: *Elizabeth Brinckerhoff.* I caught my breath as I recognized her distinctive elegant script. I could almost hear her lilting voice as I read the words:

Dear Katy,
This is a 6 pence! Save it! With a 6 pence in her shoe!
Ask Mother!
Love,
Mama B

Taped to the note was a small silver coin, a real English sixpence.

Tears filled my eyes. I knew exactly what to do. I would give Katy the purse at her engagement party, and on her wedding day, she would walk down the aisle with the sixpence in her shoe.

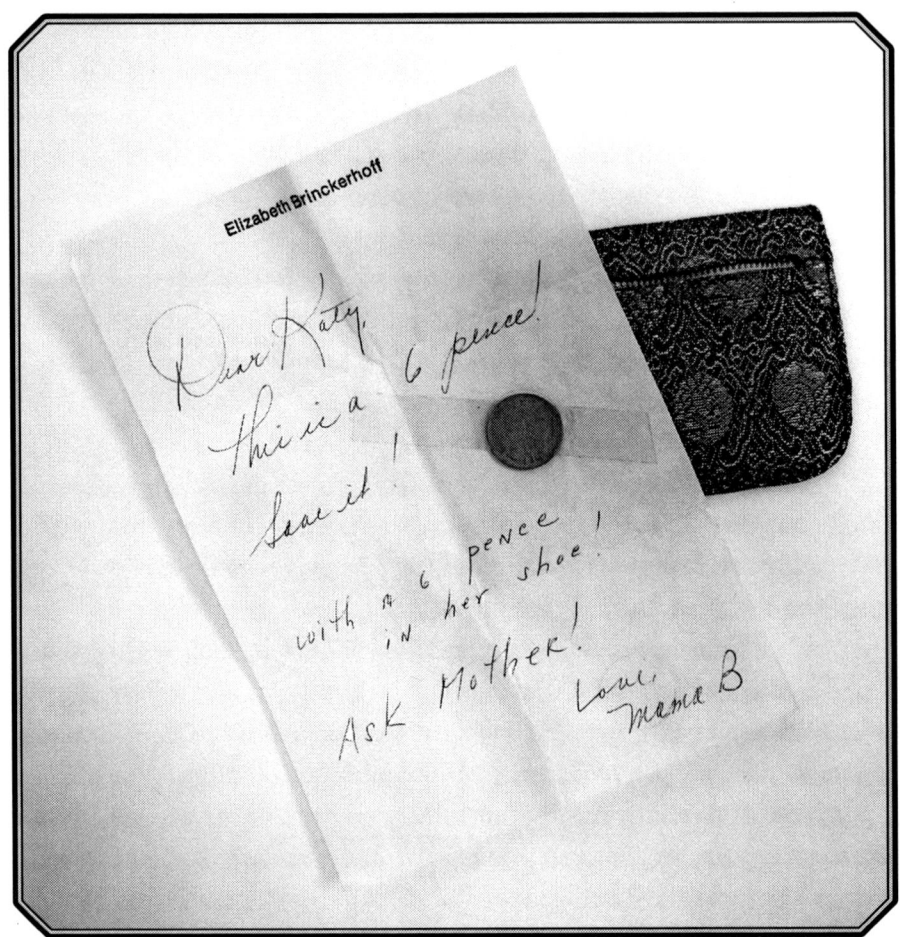

Photo credit: Kevin Eans

I carefully refolded the note, tucked it back in the purse, and gently pulled the zipper shut. My worries subsided. Joy and excitement about Katy's engagement and upcoming wedding bubbled over again.

The note had said, "Ask Mother!" The mother of the bride.

That would be me.

*Katy and me on Katy's wedding day,
February 19, 2011*

Tired of Junk E-Mails? Send This Story to Every Woman You Know!

It happens all the time. I receive an e-mail joke from someone—my sister, my friend, a friend of a friend, sometimes even my best friend—and I don't get it.

Why did she send me this joke? I wonder. *Did she think it was funny? Did the five hundred other recipients—from fancypants687@gmail.com to looneyclooney519@earthlink.com—think it was funny, too? Maybe she was bullied into sending it,* I think as I reread the last line, which inevitably (and ominously) says something along the lines of, "Do not break this e-mail chain. Forward it to ten friends—or *else!*" Or else *what?* Even in twenty-first-century cyberspace, the not-so-veiled threat of the old-fashioned chain letter lives on …

Hold on a sec. My computer just chirped. Look what's arrived! An e-mail from a friend of a friend of a friend. Talk about perfect timing.

```
>> THE DRESS
>>
>> Jennifer's wedding day was fast approaching.
>> Nothing could dampen her excitement -- not even her
>> parents' nasty divorce.
>>
>> Her mother had found the perfect dress to wear and
```

>> would be the best dressed mother-of-the-bride ever!?
>> A week later, Jennifer was horrified to learn that
>> her father's new young wife had bought the exact
>> same dress!? Jennifer asked her to exchange it, but
>> she refused. "Absolutely not. I look like a million
>> bucks in this dress, and I'm wearing it," she
>> replied.? Jennifer told her mother who graciously
>> said, "Never mind sweetheart. I'll get another
>> dress. After all it's your special day."? A few days
>> later, they went shopping and did find another
>> gorgeous dress.?
>> When they stopped for lunch, Jennifer asked her
>> mother, "Aren't you going to return the other
>> dress? You really don't have another occasion where
>> you could wear it."
>>
>> Her mother just smiled and replied, "Of course I
>> do, dear. I'm wearing it to the rehearsal dinner
>> the night before the wedding.
>>
>> NOW I ASK YOU - IS THERE A WOMAN OUT THERE,
>> *ANYWHERE*, WHO WOULDN'T ENJOY THIS STORY?? SEND IT
>> TO EVERY WOMAN YOU KNOW ! ! ! ! ! !?????? ???????

Uh-oh. I scratch my head. *Here we go again. Why did my friend of a friend of a friend (i.e.,* total stranger*) send me this? Does she really think it's funny?* I peer at the text a second time, squinting at the maddeningly tiny font, doing my best to ignore the weird spacing, excessive question marks, and annoying double arrows running down the left-hand side.

By golly, I am going to get this joke if it's the last thing I do.

Okay. Let's get the story straight. There is a girl named Jennifer. She is getting married. Her parents are recently divorced. And it's not just any divorce. It is a "nasty" divorce. This is not funny. This is sad. Initially, I am sympathetic toward the mother-of-the-bride. I suspect that this is because I have actually recently been a mother-of-the-bride. Moreover, like Jennifer's mother, I am a *woman.* Hear me roar. You go, girlfriend! Female solidarity. Sisterhood forever. Blah, blah, blah. That's what this kind of e-mail is all about, right?

Although—on second thought—*who knows* why Jennifer's parents got divorced? Maybe her father is not so bad. Maybe Jennifer's mother is not so nice. Maybe she's a control freak. A tad mean-spirited. Not much fun. You know the type. The kind of woman who shows up at her neighbor's front door and complains when you don't pick up after your dog. And even when you say you're sorry, and promise that it will never happen again, and try to explain that the reason you didn't pick up the poop was because you forgot the plastic bag, *plus* it was raining, you can tell she is *still* ticked off. *I hate it when that happens!*

But I digress.

Anyhow, there is a *dress*. I know this must be important, because the e-mail's title is "The Dress." Herein lies the crux of the story, the beating heart of the dramatic conflict: Jennifer's mother has purchased the *exact same dress* to wear at her daughter's wedding as her ex-husband's new, younger wife. Imagine that. What an amazing coincidence! I wonder if they shopped at the same store. I wonder if the two dresses are the exact same size, too. Now that would *really* be amazing!

But Jennifer is not amazed. Jennifer is "horrified."

Horrified? Isn't this perhaps a bit of an overreaction? Let's hope this drama queen is not on the path to becoming the next *Bridezilla*! When Jennifer asks her stepmother to return the dress, the stepmother refuses. Makes sense to me. Considering that the stepmother says she "looks like a million bucks" in the dress, why should she return it?

Jennifer's mother's response to this turn of events is surprisingly unruffled. "Never mind, sweetheart," she graciously replies. "I'll get another dress. After all, it's your special day."

Hold on. This response is a little *too* gracious, if you ask me.

Sure enough, a few days later, Jennifer and her mother go shopping, and her mother buys a new dress. They stop for lunch, and Jennifer asks her mother, "Aren't you going to return the other dress? You really don't have another occasion where you could wear it."

For a fleeting moment, I almost feel sorry for the woman. *No other occasion to wear a new dress? Not even one?* I would definitely feel sorry for her, if it wasn't for what she utters next—the story's punch line: "Of course I do, dear." The mother smiles. "I'm wearing it to the rehearsal dinner the night before the wedding."

I read the line again.

Yes, it is clearly the story's punch line. But I am not laughing. I picture the mother-of-the-bride's smile, and it is not a mere phony frozen smile, like Bree Van de Kamp's on *Desperate Housewives*. No. It is a crazy, evil smile!

What in the world, I wonder, *does Jennifer's mother think she will accomplish by wearing the dress to the rehearsal dinner?* For starters, everything is so casual these days. She's going to be way overdressed. Whatever. The poor woman has obviously been through a lot, what with her nasty divorce and all. I hope when she wears the dress to the rehearsal dinner that she enjoys a perfectly delightful time.

Once all the excitement of the wedding is over, maybe she can talk to someone about her anger.

My index finger hovers above the mouse, poised to click "Delete," when my eyes are drawn to the screaming all-caps, hyper-punctuated last line that crawls along the bottom of the page: "NOW I ASK YOU - IS THERE A WOMAN OUT THERE, *ANYWHERE*, WHO WOULDN'T ENJOY THIS STORY??"

At last! A question I understand. A question I can answer:

Yes! Yes, I am that woman!

Now here's an idea:

SEND THIS *STORY TO EVERY WOMAN YOU KNOW!*

Or else.

My Favorite Interview: Fred Rogers, "I Like You Just the Way You Are"

Since I have interviewed hundreds of people for *Guideposts* magazine over the past thirty-five years, people often ask me which interview was my favorite. That's easy: Fred Rogers, host of the award-winning children's television program *Mister Rogers' Neighborhood*. I hadn't been working for *Guideposts* for very long when my editor called me into his office and gave me the assignment.

"Mister Who?" I asked. I was not yet a parent and had not grown up watching this extraordinarily kind, sensitive, gentle, comforting, cardigan-wearing friend and champion of children.

The interview began like any other. We shook hands. Sat down. I had just pushed the red "record" button on my tape recorder when Mr. Rogers suddenly flipped open a tan leather briefcase and whipped out three colorful puppets—X the Owl, King Friday the Thirteenth, and Daniel Striped Tiger—and magically brought them to life! Three puppets. Two hands. Four voices. *How did he do it?*

Like a walk in the winter woods, you never know where an interview will take you … and it's the unplanned exploration of little-used overgrown side trails that so often yields the most unexpected, revealing, and delightful discoveries. Clearly Fred Rogers was a man completely at ease with himself, utterly without guile, and totally transparent. He was also a deeply spiritual man, comfortable talking about matters of faith and his relationship with God. I was surprised to learn that in addition to being the host of his television show and author of several books, he was also an ordained Presbyterian minister.

At the time of our interview, my beloved grandmother was approaching death after a long struggle with age-related dementia, and it was all I could do to maintain my composure as Mr. Rogers began to tell me about *his* beloved grandfather McFeely, who suffered in much the same way.

But I'll stop now, before I give too much away …

I Like You Just the Way You Are

by Fred Rogers

with Kathryn Brinckerhoff (Slattery)

The rain beat relentlessly against the windshield as we sped down the highway to Mercer, Pennsylvania. Mother sat next to me in the front seat. Since leaving from Pittsburgh nearly an hour ago, we had barely said a word.

It was 1952, and Ding-Dong was dying.

Ding-Dong was my grandfather, Fred Brooks McFeely, my mother's father—and one of my best friends for as long as I could remember. He earned his nickname years ago one sunny afternoon when he plunked me down on his sturdy lap to teach me the old nursery rhyme, "Ding Dong Dell." The name stuck.

I was grown up now, two years out of college and working in New York for NBC television. Just yesterday Mother had telephoned me at work with the news of Ding-Dong's illness. Well into his eighties, he'd been in a nursing home for several years. In recent months, however, his condition had worsened.

"The doctors say it's just plain old age," Mother had explained to me quietly. "They say he's fading fast." There was a long pause. "Do you think you could come home, Fred? I think we should visit him as soon as possible."

I made plans to fly from New York to Pittsburgh that evening.

In one sense, it was good to get out of the city. Lately it seemed that nothing had been going right. When I first graduated from college and arrived at NBC, I was a starry-eyed idealist—bursting with enthusiasm for the potential I felt television held not only for entertaining but for helping people. I was particularly interested in children's programming. But these were the early days of television, and there didn't seem to be much interest in such things. So my goals seemed to be shifting—and this bothered me.

I really didn't know where I was going or why. My self-confidence had sunk to near-zero. And never had I felt so far away from God.

I'd taken to stopping by St. Patrick's Cathedral on Fifth Avenue for morning prayer before going to work. Mostly, I prayed for guidance. But I was still uncertain and confused ...

"Fred," my mother interrupted my thoughts as our car continued on the slick highway. "He might not know you."

"What?" I asked.

"Your grandfather," she answered. "He's all mixed-up. He doesn't know what day it is. Sometimes he doesn't even know where he is."

I felt my throat tighten. Poor Ding-Dong.

"But he is happy," Mother went on. "And he loves to watch television."

"He does?"

"Yes, he loves to watch TV—especially *The Kate Smith Hour*. He knows that's one of the shows you work on. And from what I gather, he's forever telling everyone in the home about his grandson in New York City. He's so proud of you, Fred. You're special to him. You always have been, you know."

I nodded silently. Listening to the rhythmic sound of the windshield wipers, I let my thoughts travel back to childhood ...

As a youngster, there was nothing I liked better than Sunday afternoons at Ding-Dong's rambling farm in western Pennsylvania. Surrounded by miles of winding stone walls, the rustic house and red brick barn provided endless hours of fun and discovery for a city kid like me. I was used to neat-as-a-pin parlors with porcelain figures that seemed to whisper, "Not to be touched!" ... to clean, starched shirts and neatly combed hair warning, "Not to be mussed!" ... and to the inevitable wagging of an adult's "Don't do that, you might hurt yourself!" finger.

I could still remember vividly one afternoon when I was eight years old. Since my very first visit to the farm, I'd wanted more than anything to be allowed to climb the network of stone walls surrounding the property. My parents would never approve. The walls were old; some stones were missing, others loose and crumbling. Still, my yearning to scramble across those walls the way I'd watched other boys do grew so strong that finally, one spring afternoon, I summoned all my courage and entered the drawing room where the adults had gathered after Sunday dinner.

All were chatting softly, sipping cups of tea and coffee. I cleared my throat. No one seemed to notice me.

"Hey," I said hesitantly.

Everyone noticed me.

"I, uh—I wanna climb the stone walls," I said. "Can I climb the stone walls?"

Instantly a chorus went up from the women in the room.

"Heavens, no!" they cried in dismay. "You'll hurt yourself!"

I wasn't really disappointed. The response was just as I'd expected. But before I could leave the room, I was stopped by Ding-Dong's booming voice.

"Now hold on just a minute," I heard him say. "So the boy wants to climb the stone walls? Then let the boy climb the walls! He has to learn to do things for himself.

"Now scoot on out of here," he said to me with a wink. "And come see me when you get back."

"Yes, sir," I stammered, my heart pounding with excitement.

For the next two and a half hours, I climbed those old walls, skinned my knee, tore my pants, and had the time of my life. Later, when I met with Ding-Dong to tell him about my adventures, he said words I never forgot.

"Fred," he grinned, "you made this day a special day just by being yourself. Always remember, there's just one person in this whole world like you—and I like you just the way you are."

I wondered now if he ever knew how important that day—and his words—had been to me. I wondered if there was any way I could ever repay him.

The rain was letting up as we drove down the main drive to the neat clapboard cottage where Ding-Dong stayed. A white-uniformed nurse answered the door. "Mr. McFeely's had a nice day," she said as she let us in. "He's watching TV now. Kate Smith's show is on. It's his favorite program."

"Ding-Dong?" I said, peering into the dimly lit room. He was sitting in a chair next to the bed.

"Ding-Dong?" I hardly recognized him. He was so tiny, so frail and bent. He lifted his head.

"Hello," he said, extending a feeble hand. "Hello, young man. Have a seat." He motioned to a nearby chair. "Have a seat," he repeated, "and watch this show with me. This is Kate Smith. This is a fine show."

I sat in the chair and watched the program. On my grandfather's nightstand was a framed photo of the two of us. When the commercial came on, Ding-Dong said, "You know, young man, this television's a mighty great invention. I've got a grandson in New York, and he told me all about it. He's something, that boy. And he's going to do great things in television. Yes, he is."

Ding-Dong was smiling, his blue eyes twinkling ever so faintly.

"Yes," he went on, "I've got quite a grandson." He gestured toward the photo on his nightstand. "Would you like to meet him?"

It was obvious Ding-Dong didn't recognize me. But that was all right with me. Wherever in time or place Ding-Dong was in his weary old mind, I just wanted to let him be. All I could hear were his own words echoing in my head: *There's just one person in the whole world like you. And I like you just the way you are.*

"That's some grandson you've got," I said. "You know, I believe he is going to try to do good things in television. He sure cares a lot about you. You've helped him understand some of the most important things in life."

Ding-Dong smiled and nodded. He seemed very happy, but he was tired. He asked to be put to bed. The nurse helped him up from his chair. Mother and I tucked him in. We chatted a bit more and then sat quietly until he fell asleep.

On the way home, we were silent. But I felt strangely happy inside—somehow peaceful. Something very special had happened that afternoon. In a very personal way, God had answered my prayers.

I was beginning to understand what it was He wanted me to do with my television career: He wanted me to offer children the same kind of reassurance, encouragement, and sense of self-worth that Ding-Dong had given me. I didn't know exactly how or when the right opportunities would arise, but I felt confident now that I would be ready to meet them.

A few weeks later, I received an invitation to leave New York and join a small educational television station in Pittsburgh that was looking for a person to develop new programming. I jumped at the chance. And it was from those small beginnings—hand-built sets, props, and puppets—that the themes and characters that now populate *Mister Rogers' Neighborhood* evolved.

That was twenty-six years ago. Today, through the wonder of television, *Mister Rogers' Neighborhood* is visited each day by millions of children throughout America and other lands. There have been changes over the years; characters and special guests to the Neighborhood come and go. But one thing—my message to the children at the close of every show—remains the same.

"There's just one person in the whole world like you," the kids can count on hearing me say. "And people can like you just the way you are."

Ding-Dong, I know, would agree.

What's Your Story? Kitty's Writing Tips

If you are reading this chapter, then you are interested in writing. How exciting! Whether you're nine or ninety years old, here is good news: Writing is *good for you*!

Perhaps like you, I often write for very practical purposes. This is because writing helps me think more clearly. When wrestling with a decision, here's a tried-and-true tip my father taught me years ago: Take a piece of paper, draw a line down the middle, and list the pros of the issue on one side and the cons on the other. You would be amazed how this can help with day-to-day problem solving!

Other times, when I am struggling with a difficult situation and I don't know how to pray, I write God a letter. In the process, God often encourages me, gives me insights, and gently shows me the way. When I find myself worrying yet again about the situation (which I am prone to do!), I am able to reread my letter to God and once again am encouraged and grounded in faith.

And of course there are those times when creative writing allows our imaginations to take flight. As I mentioned at the beginning of this book, we are all storytellers. It's part of what makes us human. There's a reason God made us this way. When we choose to step out in faith and share our stories, beautiful and amazing things can happen. God uses our stories—our heart songs—to help each other as we travel along life's journey.

Perhaps like you, when I get an idea for an article or book, I get so excited that I drop whatever I'm doing and scribble it down. Thank heavens for sticky notes! When I am working on an article or book, I find myself thinking about it all day long. I go to bed thinking about it and dream about it at night.

Did you know that when you are sleeping, your subconscious brain keeps on solving problems and coming up with new ideas? Sometimes in the middle of the night—and many mornings—I wake up with my mind brimming with fresh ideas. *Keeping a pad and pencil by the bed comes in handy on these occasions.*

Like any task, one of the hardest things about writing is getting started. I think you will probably agree that there is nothing quite so intimidating as a blank computer screen! *That's why each time I sit down at the computer and place my hands on the keyboard, I say a little prayer.* I thank God for the opportunity to write. Then I ask Him to guide and inspire me as I work. A short prayer not only helps me to focus on the task ahead but also serves to encourage me and take away my fear. It also helps to prevent "writer's block," which is nothing more than a fancy name for procrastination.

Some people tend to romanticize writing. By "romanticize," I mean that some people think of writing as a purely artistic endeavor, and they think of writers as being uniquely "talented" or "gifted." *The truth is, writing is a skill. And like any skill, the more you write, the better you write.* True, like being able to draw or carry a tune, the ability to string words, sentences, and paragraphs together can be an innate aptitude. Yes, there can be wonderful moments in the creative process where you "lose time" and are utterly astounded at the words that, out of nowhere, suddenly appear on the page. *But there is also a lot of truth to the old saying that good writing (like so many good things) is "90 percent perspiration and 10 percent inspiration."* One of my favorite writers, the late Madeleine L'Engle, summed up her experience of the writing process this way: "Inspiration usually comes *during* work, rather than before it."

Once you sit down and start writing, the words will come—I promise!—sometimes slowly and sometimes pouring out like a fountain. Once you start, there will be no turning back. Like an unfinished jigsaw puzzle, each day your manuscript will be waiting for you to find the missing pieces and complete the beautiful picture.

After you think your article or story is finished, it is a good idea to give it plenty of time—at least a day or two—to "cool down." The sense of elation experienced after completing a manuscript can be so euphoric that the urge to dash your masterpiece off to an editor or publisher can be nearly irresistible. *Don't do it!* You will be amazed how many typos can hide in a just-completed manuscript. Letting a hot manuscript cool also gives you time to make other revisions and almost always results in a much-improved final version.

Bottom line: *Every writer will tell you the secret to* good *writing is ... * rewriting*!*

In the end, writing is work—hard work. When it comes to the writing process, I guess I'm a little bit like Dorothy Parker, who once quipped, "I hate writing. But I *love* having written."

Finally, when it comes to writing, here is the most important thing to remember: *Only you can tell your story the way you want to tell it. No one else can do the job like you. No one!* Regarding getting published, I firmly believe that if getting a story, or book, into the hands of readers is something that God wants for His good purposes, then *nothing* can stop it from happening. *Nothing!*

So gather up your ideas, find a quiet spot, and start writing!

Heart Song

As I rise from nighttime's slumber

Blessed with grace and joy and wonder

Be with me now, O Lord, I pray

And thank You for this glorious day!

About the Author

Kathryn Slattery has written hundreds of stories of hope and inspiration for a wide variety of publications, including *ParentLife*, *Today's Christian Woman*, and *Angels on Earth* magazines, and she is a long-time contributing editor for *Guideposts* magazine.

In addition to *Heart Songs: A Family Treasury of True Stories of Hope and Inspiration*, she is the author of the memoir *Lost & Found: One Daughter's Story of Amazing Grace* (GuidepostsBooks), *If I Could Ask God Anything: Awesome Bible Answers for Curious Kids* (Thomas Nelson), *Grandma, I'll Miss You: A Child's Story about Death and New Life* (David C. Cook), *The Grace To Grow: The Power of Christian Faith in Emotional Healing*, and *A Bright-Shining Place: The Story of a Miracle*, and she is a contributing author to numerous *Guideposts* anthologies. Her popular children's book *The Gospel for Kids* (David C. Cook) has more than one hundred thousand copies in print in nine languages. Kathryn is also the author of the "Kids' Question of the Week" blog on TommyNelson.com.

Kathryn, who is known as "Kitty," resides in Connecticut with her husband, Tom, where they are the parents of two grown children and happy owners of a roly-poly pug named Max. Visit Kitty and learn more about her work at her website: www.KathrynSlattery.com, and her Facebook Author Page: Kathryn "Kitty" Slattery.